100 TALKS
FOR ALL-AGE WORSHIP

SUSAN SAYERS

Kevin
Mayhew

Rainbows and pro'
1 is our best

First published in 1997 by
KEVIN MAYHEW LTD
Buxhall
Stowmarket
Suffolk IP14 3BW

© 1997 Kevin Mayhew Ltd

The right of Susan Sayers to be identified as the author
of this work has been asserted by her in accordance
with the Copyright, Designs and Patents Act 1988.

ISBN 1 84003 056 9
Catalogue No 1500141

2 3 4 5 6 7 8 9

Cover illustration: *Family of five* by Diana Ong
Reproduced by courtesy of SuperStock, London

Cover design by Jaquetta Sergeant
Edited by Peter Dainty
Typesetting by Louise Hill
Printed and bound in Great Britain

Contents

FAMILY AND NEIGHBOURS

Foreword

It is common practice in modern churches for the whole church family, from the youngest to the oldest, to come together for at least part of morning worship. This may be for a few minutes at the beginning or ending of the service, but there will also be times when the whole of worship is shared by all ages. One of the most challenging and potentially exciting aspects of such worship is the opportunity it provides for the proclamation of the Gospel and the presentation of Christian teaching in stimulating and refreshing ways.

Anyone who has had the privilege of leading all-age worship will be aware not only of its difficulties, but also of its delights – one of which is the strong sense of *sharing* which is sometimes missing from more formal worship patterns. For one thing, there is a shared understanding of the teaching. The Gospel is for all, and can be understood by all when it is expressed in terms of everyday experiences to which everyone can relate at their own level. Jesus himself knew this, and that is one of the reasons why he taught in parables. The ideas in this book aim to present the Gospel message in a way that will mean something to every member of the congregation. The shared understanding which results will have an untold spiritual impact on the corporate life of the church.

Another delight of all-age worship springs from shared participation in the teaching. Movement, speech and action are encouraged; in fact they are essential if the congregation is to feel involved, not only superficially but at a deeper level. Humour will play an important part, but more important will be the greater sense of togetherness and mutual awareness which a more open and uninhibited expression of faith and feeling make possible.

The ideas presented here are only suggestions, of course, and it is to be hoped that they will be adapted to suit the needs of particular churches, or that they will inspire other ideas which will present the Christian message in ways that are both memorable and meaningful. Expect the unexpected

– the Holy Spirit can speak to us not only through the carefully prepared words of the minister or leader, but also through the uninhibited comments and actions of children and adults alike, who are learning together what God has to say to his people.

SUSAN SAYERS

THE TRUE GOD

In charge

Beforehand, collect together one of those cocktail stick umbrellas for decorating drinks, a small/child's umbrella and a huge golfing umbrella.

You will also need to make a crossing patrol lollipop, out of card fixed to a broom handle or bamboo cane.

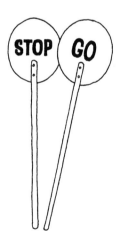

Begin by setting up the centre aisle as a road with a crossing patrol at it. A group of children show how it works, while the rest of the congregation watch or make traffic noises.

Ask who was in charge in that situation. How do we know? What might happen if the lollipop man/lady wasn't in charge?

Explain that lots of people are in charge. Perhaps some of the people here are in charge of people at their work, in charge of certain jobs at home, or in charge of looking after a person or a pet. When we're in charge we can sometimes get bossy, and think we have lots of power. Sometimes we use our power of being in charge to do what is wrong – as when people are put in charge of money and fiddle the books to steal the money, or when powerful leaders of a country use their power to make themselves very rich while the poor in their country starve. And that is wrong.

The one who is in charge over everything is God. Even when we are put in charge, God is in charge over us. Some people think God's power is no bigger over them than this. (Put the cocktail umbrella up over someone's head.) So they get bossy and greedy, and don't bother about what is a right, caring way to be in charge. Some people think God is in charge, but only about this much. (Put the small umbrella up over someone's head.) So they act responsibly some of the time, but if they feel like using their power badly, and don't think they'll be found out, they go ahead. But other people know that however important they get in life, it's God who is really in charge totally and completely. (Put up the golfing umbrella over someone small.) So when they are put in charge of anyone or anything they do it God's way – in a caring, honest and humble way.

Describing God

Begin by asking a couple of volunteers to take part in a guessing game. Give one person a note with the name of an animal written on it. This person tries to describe the animal to the other person, who has to guess what the animal is. If you have access to an OHP or flip chart you could get the second person to draw what they hear being described. You could have two or three goes at this, or you could ask everyone in the congregation to pair up and play the game. The way you do it will depend on the expectations and nature of the congregation!

Now fix a cardboard pair of rabbit ears on a volunteer and explain how we all tend to describe things in terms of what we know already. We would probably describe a rabbit as being furry with long ears because our own ears are short, and we are generally lacking in fur. Ask for suggestions as to how a rabbit might describe a human? (It might be something like a bald rabbit with very short ears.)

It's even harder trying to describe someone we have never seen, like God. It's difficult, but we do our best by looking at the world he has created and picking up clues from this. What can we tell about God by (a) looking at his creation? (Write these qualities up for everyone to see.) (b) Looking at Jesus? (Write these qualities too.) (c) Looking at the working of the Holy Spirit? (Add these qualities.)

When we worship the Trinity we are remembering all these qualities in the God we love.

Idolatry

Ask for four volunteers to carry four objects in procession from the back of the building, so that everyone can see them as they go past. There is a charm bracelet, or some other superstitious thing; a mirror; a clock; and a wallet. Have the objects displayed at the front.

Explain how God has warned us to be on our guard in case we are tempted to worship other things instead of the one true God. Sometimes we don't realise when we are doing this, so today we are going to check our lives to make sure we really are worshipping God, and not some idol. We may not kneel down in front of trees or golden calves, but these objects give us a clue as to some other ways we may be just as full of idolatry.

Look at each object in turn. The charm bracelet: believing in luck ruling our lives, with the sense that there is no real order or point in it. God is there, but not actually able to do much.

The mirror: our image becomes extremely important to us. It is more vital to do/wear/have the same as everyone else than to be what God wants and plans us to be.

The clock: feeling that we are only valuable if our diary is full and we have to organise every second of our day. We have effectively blocked God from using our time, except for a little space which we control.

The wallet: we love our possessions and comforts, and forget that as Christians we are no longer owners of anything, but stewards.

As the objects are slowly paraded again, ask people to think carefully as to whether any of them have become idols, and ask God to sort their lives out again.

False images

We all have different images of the people we know and each person is actually all these and more. As we get to know a person better, we keep adjusting our image of them.

As we get to know God better we shall find the same thing – we will gradually be putting right any false images we have of him and be more able to love and worship him as he really is. Sometimes our false images of God have been handed down to us by how we were first introduced. There are empty seats here now because some people in our area have rejected what is in fact a false image of God and one of our main tasks is to show people the true God.

Let's look at some of these commonly held false images:

This god is always ready to condemn us and is very severe, very demanding and disapproves of us enjoying ourselves.

This god made the world a long time ago and then lost interest. He's actually rather lazy and lets us get on with destroying ourselves.

This god is rather pathetic; he smiles naively and doesn't understand the real world that we have to cope with. If you ask him for help he'd probably say he'd like to but it's all rather difficult with things as they are.

This god picks on people and makes life terrible for them.

This god is a little slave-magician, who runs round doing everything we ask but is somewhat deaf and forgetful.

Let's be quite clear about this: all these gods are false images and are nothing at all like the true and living God. We need to destroy them. (Either cross them all out or, if you are using paper, tear them up and throw them away.) Thank goodness people who have these images often do reject them. How tragic that they think God is like that – no wonder people decide not to worship him.

So what is our God really like? Write 'The true God is . . .' in the centre and have people adding to the qualities they have discovered him to be.

Designer gods

As people come into church, give them all a pipe cleaner and a piece of string. Begin the talk by asking everyone to design an animal of some kind using the pipe cleaner and string provided. Everyone can hold up their masterpieces for general admiration.

Point out that everyone's creation is different because we all had our own ideas. We might have picked up on certain qualities of real animals, but even the best of our creations is not much like any real animal we might know.

People invent gods to worship rather as we made our animals. Sometimes there are aspects in these gods which are like the real God, but they are not really anything like the one true God who loved us all into being and is the beginning and end of all things.

We cannot pick and choose with God, making him as we feel on any particular day; we cannot make him at all, because he is there already and always has been. What we can do is enjoy him as he is, enjoy him loving us, and enjoy getting to know him better and better.

God is not a robot

If possible, beg or borrow a radio-controlled car for today. If you don't know anyone who owns such a thing devise one using a willing child, and a carton which she holds round her middle like this:

Tell the controlled car (in either version) which way you want it to go and see how it does exactly what you tell it. Parents wish they could do it to their children! Children wish they could do it to their teachers! And sometimes that's the way we treat God – we might say, 'Well, I don't believe in God any more because I asked him to get me a bike and he didn't'. That doesn't prove that God isn't there – it proves that God isn't a radio-controlled car or a slot machine or a magic lamp! And that's true. He isn't.

God certainly comes among us as one who serves, but we mustn't presume to take him out of a box in emergencies. God is not our slave, and his way of doing things is much better than ours anyway, because he understands the whole situation and all the people involved. He's rather like a conductor or composer, bringing all the different parts of the orchestra together to make a beautiful harmony.

So what have we learnt today?

- that we can't control God
- that God is in control
- but that God never makes us do what he wants; we are free to choose.

Worshipping the real God

You will need a loaded camera with a built-in light meter and flash. Begin by introducing everyone to your camera and taking two or three photos, focusing on different people and parts of the building each time. Explain that you don't need lots of complicated flash equipment with this camera because it has been designed with the light meter and flash facility built in. That means that whenever you go to take a picture, the camera automatically checks the light and provides extra light if necessary.

God has designed us with a built-in worship facility. Of course the idea is that we use this to worship our maker and, when we do that, the rest of our life settles into a fully satisfying 'rightness' which is good and liberating. But the facility is still there, whether we use it like this or not and we all worship something because that is part of our design. The real question is 'what'?

Look again at the camera as it focuses on a particular person or thing to photograph. I may insist that I'm trying to get a picture of the organist, but if I'm actually focusing on Brown Owl, then that's the actual picture I'm taking and that's the picture I'll get. (Take the picture.) We may say we worship God, but if our hearts and minds are focused mostly on what we look like and wear, or on food, or the luxury bathroom we'd like, or our hobby, or our girl/ boyfriends, or work, then the truth is that we are actually worshipping these things, and not God at all.

Today God is reminding us that all these other idols are very poor substitutes for the real thing; let's get our priorities right if the focus has slipped, and really enjoy using our worship facility in the way it was designed to be used – worshipping the God of enormous power who can work wonders in our characters; the God who has always loved us and cherished us right from our conception onwards; the God who loves and honours us even when our hair goes grey and we aren't as fit as we used to be. This God can provide everything we ever need; let's focus our worship on him alone.

Getting to know God

Begin by talking about how first impressions are sometimes spot on, and sometimes disastrously wrong. We gradually get to know who someone really is by the clues their words and behaviour give us.

Ask a volunteer (of 12 years or over) to come and help. Secretly show them the picture of what they are and then hang the picture on their back so that no one can see it. Invite everyone to ask the volunteer questions to which s/he can only answer 'yes' or 'no'. Keep track of what is found out until eventually the identity is guessed correctly and the volunteer turns round to reveal that s/he is indeed who they thought.

What on earth has this to do with our theme?

The fact is that we get to know Jesus in exactly the same way – bit by bit we start to discover his character by seeing how he acts towards people in the Gospel. Bit by bit we learn that he is revealing God's nature to us, until eventually we can say for certain that he truly is the Son of God.

It's the same with our experience of the living God. Gradually as we keep in close touch with him we get to know him better and recognise wonders in our lives which are typically God's doing. Perhaps we've been praying and praying for God to sort out a problem, and then events start coming together in a way which is totally different from what we had in mind, but solves the problem in a better way than we could have hoped for. And we thank God very fondly and affectionately, because we recognise that it has been a typical God-response to our need, and we have got to know him better in the process.

But we must seek him; we would never have found out who the volunteer was unless we had asked and used our curiosity and imagination. If we walk through this week more alert, attentive and expectant, we shall notice the signs of glory we may have been missing.

The mind of God

Beforehand make three large card signs on which are written: GOD MIND S.

First ask three volunteers to hold the signs up in this order: GODS MIND and explain that this morning we are going to think about the way God's mind works: how God thinks.

Ask if anyone knows what you are thinking. They might be able to guess, but really our thoughts are very secret, unless we choose to give people clues to how we're thinking. Mime being angry about the choice of one of today's hymns, and see if anyone can then work out from this what is in your mind. Then mime something which shows you are pleased or surprised. (These could all be linked with the hymn numbers if you wish.)

Explain that God does want us to understand what's in his mind, so he gives us clues which we see in the things he has made. We know from the way the universe works, for instance, that God must be very careful and imaginative, enjoy lots of variety, like order and harmony, and consider everything important, from the largest to the tiniest item.

Ask the volunteers to rearrange themselves so that the message now reads: GOD MINDS. God cares about us and all his creation; he bothers about how we are feeling and what we are doing. He hurts when we hurt and aches when we mess our lives up for ourselves and those close to us. He is overjoyed when we find real happiness and delight with him in the way things are designed to be. If we want people to be really clear about what is in our mind, we talk, and explain how we are feeling and what we are thinking. And God does that, too. Jesus is often called the Word of God, and through Jesus' words we can find out clearly what is in God's mind. All through the gospel we get the message that God minds. He knows everything we think and say and do, and minds about it.

Standing with God

Ask if anyone is brave enough to stand up on their own and say, 'I am a Christian'. Have a few people from different ages to do this and recognise that we don't find it easy to stand up on our own and admit our faith, even here among friends. No wonder we find it so hard to stand up and say what we believe when we are among people who disagree, sneer at God, or may think we're weird.

Ask three people to come and stand out in front while everyone else suddenly stands up and points at them. We often feel like them – very small and vulnerable – when we find ourselves the only Christians around, or when we are feeling very strongly tempted to do wrong, and so we keep quiet when we could be speaking out against evil, or we try and avoid going where our faith will be challenged.

But what did the prophet say to the King of Israel (1 Kings 20:28)? (Display these words: 'I will deliver this vast army into your hands, and you will know that I am the Lord'.) Have all the people to be the prophet and whisper these words to the few in the front. Emphasise that these words are true; we are fighting against evil and the evil is certainly powerful, but we are fighting in the power of God, who is far more powerful and in his strength we can be brave.

God speaks our language

Beforehand ask a couple of computer crazy people to work out a very short conversation using as much jargon as they can fit in. If you have any Latin or Greek scholars, ask them to work out a brief conversation in that language, and if you have a couple of teachers, ask them to do a short discussion using all the technical attainment targets jargon. Of course you may have different skills and interests among your congregation, so home in on any kind of language which means everything to those in the know and nothing whatever to anyone else.

Begin by introducing the two or three conversations as if they are really going to help people. Then admit that you haven't actually understood very much yourself, and no doubt they haven't either. Language can sometimes block our understanding; church language can sometimes make visitors feel like aliens visiting a strange planet, if it is too different from ordinary language that we use every day. Some of the older translations of the Bible, though beautiful to those who have grown up with them, can make a new reader suppose that Jesus has nothing in common with their own time, and only speaks in a language they don't understand.

But of course that isn't true. Jesus spoke to the woman at the well in a way that she understood so clearly that she shot off and dragged all her friends along to meet him (John 4).

When God makes himself known to you it will be in a way that you, personally, understand, because he knows you and loves you. He knows what makes you tick, what you are afraid of, what you hate doing and what you enjoy. He knows what you've been through in your life, what you can cope with easily and what you find very hard. So as he walks with you through each moment of each day right through death and beyond, he will explain things to you, comfort you and give you a nudge in ways which exactly suit your character and situation. All we have to do is live each day expecting him to be in touch, so that we recognise his voice.

He may speak during your prayer time by ideas that suddenly come and will solve a problem in a way you hadn't thought of before. He may speak by something from your Bible reading suddenly hitting you with fresh and very personal meaning. He may speak through events that happen through the day, so that you understand them as picture language which God uses to teach you something he wanted you to learn or understand. He may speak through a conversation you have, or even overhear.

So often, though, God takes us by surprise, and we need to be prepared for that in case we think it can't be God because he's not following our rules. God made this whole universe, so nothing at all is unusable. Keep your ears open, then, and be ready to listen whenever your God speaks.

GOD OUR HELPER

Living in God's strength

Have a very large, heavy suitcase or box, and make up a short, preferably funny, reason for it being there. Explain that it's extremely important to get this thing moved to the back of the church (or even up to the balcony, if you have one). Invite a small person to come out. Who thinks this person will be able to do it? Let them try, but intervene before any ruptures threaten! What we need is someone really strong. If there are any weightlifters among the uniformed organisations, now is the time for them to be put to the test.

Everyone watches as strength (or combined strength if necessary) achieves the desired effect.

In our lives we often find we have heavy weights to carry. Weights like being left out of the group at school; missing someone we love because they have moved away or died; weights like financial problems, illness or guilt about something we did years ago. (You could have heavy dustbin bags to represent all these.) We find them difficult because we try to lift them with our own strength and all we do is strain ourselves.

Our God is so powerful – he has all the strength needed to carry any weight, no matter how heavy. So the obvious, sensible thing is to let him. Stop saying to God, 'No thanks, I'm fine . . . I'll manage . . .' Stop saying to God, 'You lived ages ago, and I need help now!' Jesus *is* alive right now, full of power, full of good ideas, full of sympathy and understanding. He loves you, he knows your burden already, and he's happy to carry it so you can be free of it.

God to the rescue

You will need a fairly large globe. You may choose to use a few slides of stars and planets (and a projector) as well.

Begin by talking about those times when you're watching a quiz programme or a football match and the people you are watching are making terrible mistakes. You may shout advice at them on the telly, but they don't seem to take any notice of you!

I suspect that might be a little like God feels, as he watches the people he has made messing up their own and other people's lives, and taking not a blind bit of notice of him, even though he could make their lives so much richer and more peaceful.

Now show some pictures of the extent of God's majesty and/or the globe, getting people's help with naming the other planets in our solar system, the name of our sun and our galaxy. Aim to get across the size, beauty and order of God's creation and therefore of the creator himself.

Use the globe to look at the littleness of our world and the separate countries. God has made us free to choose good and evil, and we were getting ourselves and each other into a mess we couldn't get out of. God was prepared to lay all that greatness and majesty aside so as to rescue us by being born, and walking around as a human, loving us back to freedom again.

God's protection

You will need a couple of baby care items, designed for the child's protection (such as a playpen, stairgate, reins or baby alarm). You will also need large signs saying: EGYPT, BETHLEHEM and NAZARETH.

First show everyone the items you have brought, and ask some parents and babies to demonstrate how they are used, reminding people as they watch those aged two and under that Jesus was about this age when Herod's soldiers came to kill him.

Parents spend a lot of effort making sure that their young are safe – as we get older we sometimes think they're fusspots, but their concern for our safety grows out of their love for us. It is because God, our parent, loves us so much that he promises to look after us for ever. Now ask for three volunteers to be Joseph, Mary and Jesus (young toddler) – preferably a family. Ask three other people to be road signs, standing in different parts of the building. (You could use a balcony for Egypt, if there is one.)

Ask the family to start at Bethlehem. King Herod felt threatened by this small boy, so God kept him safe by having him in a family and warning Joseph of the danger of staying in Bethlehem. Joseph listened and acted straight away, rushing his family off to Egypt. (They rush to Egypt.) While they were there Herod died, but his successor was just as cruel so they didn't go back to Bethlehem, they went to Nazareth, which is where they settled.

God may be trying to use us as part of someone's rescue plan. He won't be able to unless we listen to him and do what he wants, whether we understand the reasons or not.

By God's grace we are able

You will need a bowl, a potato and an efficient potato peeler, or several sets of these things if the congregation is large.

First arrange for people with bowls and potatoes (but no peelers yet) to stand at intervals around the building, so that everyone can see what's going on. The volunteers can be of any age – a mixture of ages is best.

Now tell everyone that these people have been given an important job to do; they have to peel a potato and they can start straight away. When they can't start because they have no peeler, tell them to use a coin or a key, a credit card or anything they happen to have brought with them. If they can't find anything at all to use they'll have to use their finger nails. After giving them a little time to struggle, point out how we often struggle to live as Christians relying on whatever we happen to have handy, and so we make heavy weather of loving our enemies, forgiving one another or accepting criticism. Actually God never asks us to work at anything without supplying us with the grace we need. Ask if a potato peeler would make this job easier and give out the peelers.

Now they can do a far more effective job, with far less struggle. We will all lead far more effective lives, which show God's glory, if we are open to God and take time to receive his grace, rather than rushing in to work in our own strength. Ask them to put the peeled potatoes in a bowl of water near the door, to remind us as we go out of church that we need God's grace if our lives are to shine with his glory.

God's refreshing love

Bring in some plants in pots, some of which are wilting pretty badly for need of a good soaking. Choose the kind of plants which respond quickly to kind treatment. You will also need a watering can. Place some of the plants in awkward, hidden places in the building.

Begin by displaying your good, healthy plants, and contrast them with the sad-looking ones. Explain how we sometimes feel spiritually dry and thirsty, sometimes wilting in the stress of a deep worry, or something sad happening in our lives.

God is like a gardener who loves his plants – he sees us wilting and comes to pour his love and hope into our lives again. (Water the plants.) Some plants are easy to water, but others, like us, get themselves in really awkward places, miles from the water and difficult to get at. But God doesn't leave them to go on wilting, he goes out to find them and takes lots of trouble to get at them because he loves them, and wants them to be full of life. (Go around watering the other plants.

There is no area of your life or our world which is beyond the refreshing touch of the loving, powerful God. (Stand all the plants where they can be seen through the service, so that by the end they can be seen to have brightened up.)

In God's hands

First ask for two volunteers to take part in a memory game. Explain that you will reel off a list of numbers and then see how many people in church can remember the list. The two volunteers are given biro pens and told to write the numbers down on the palm of their hands as you say them. When you ask if anyone can tell you the numbers, probably the only ones able to will be those who had written the numbers on their hand to remind them.

Isaiah 49:13-16 explains that God never forgets us – it is as if he has our name written on the palm of his hand, so that he is always lovingly calling us to mind. What God offers us is the chance to be yoked up with him as we stumble and plod our way through life. Show everyone a cut-out yoke, and explain how it worked, with the stronger, more experienced animal helping to guide the younger one in the right way so that the load is less painful to carry.

Finding God's help

Beforehand collect four shoe boxes, and in one of them place a pair of binoculars. Ask a volunteer who wears glasses to help you with the talk this morning. Ask her to stand where most people can see her, and put a chair at four points round her, not near enough for her to touch. Blindfold the volunteer, or ask her to close her eyes. On each of the chairs place a box, and in the box containing binoculars place her glasses. Turn her to face another chair. Point out that Helen needs her glasses, and life is very difficult without them. She can't see much (even when she's not wearing a blindfold!) and she feels very vulnerable. We may feel like this if we suddenly lose something important to us. Perhaps our best friend moves, or we lose our job, or we have a row at home, and suddenly we don't know exactly who we are or which way to turn.

The secret is to turn in the right direction, because God is the one who has both power and inclination to help. His motive is ardent love for his precious child. If we turn any other way and walk in that direction, we will face emptiness and disappointment. (Help Helen to turn in each wrong direction, open the shoe box and find nothing.) But if we turn in the right direction – turn towards God and walk his way (turn Helen the right way), then we will find fulfilment, often far more than we dared hope for. (Helen opens the box and finds in it not only her glasses but a pair of binoculars as well.)

With God in danger

You will need a climbing rope and a life jacket, or some other equipment which protects you from danger in dangerous hobbies. Also a DANGER sign.

First show the equipment, talking about what mad things climbers and slalom canoeists get up to. Ask for a show of hands as to who reckons each is a dangerous hobby. Those who do such things rely on their equipment to protect them, even when they are in acute danger. (If you have any free-fallers, white-water enthusiasts, etc., you could interview them briefly about their most scary moment.)

God is our life-line. He is our sure protection when we are living dangerously in his service, and whatever happens to us (even death), we know that we shall be safe in his hands.

What if we roped up together and then walked down the high street, or put on life jackets and then proceeded to do the washing up? It would be ridiculous, wouldn't it! But sometimes we behave like that – we come to church and offer our whole life to God, sing his praise and pray for the world, then go home and live as safely as we can, keeping our faith as quiet as possible and not getting involved with any evangelism if we can help it.

Let's think again: God promises his protection and we love him, so let's take our courage in both hands and really make ourselves available for him to use in whatever ugly situations he may need us to be.

Accepting God's help

Begin with the sketch set out below. After the sketch ask people to say what they thought the sketch was about. Ideas may well come from this which you and I haven't thought of. That is excellent; they may be issues which people in your congregation need to hear. Draw the ideas together – unless we accept our need of help, God can't help us. All the time we reckon there's nothing wrong with us we don't go to a doctor; it's only when we recognise our need of spiritual healing that we start valuing Jesus and listening attentively to what he says.

Drama sketch: At the doctor's.

Have a sign up with the doctor's name on it and the doctor wearing a stethoscope.

A patient walks in with wads of cotton wool plastered over his eyes so that he can barely see. He gropes around, bumping into the wall, and finds his way to the chair, with the doctor guiding him, something like this:

Doc   Ah, good morning, Mr Henning! Do take a seat . . . no, that's the table . . . the seat's over to the right a bit.

Patient   Alright, alright, I know where I'm going. What do you think I am . . . blind or something?

Doc   Now how can I help you?

Patient   Help me? How on earth would you be able to help me? Anyone would think there was something wrong with me!

Doc   Er . . . Perhaps I could examine your eyes?

Patient   *(jumping up)* Oh no you don't! I've heard about people like you. As if I'd trust my eyes to your interfering fingers. They're my own eyes, aren't they?

Doc   Well yes, of course, but . . .

Patient   There you are then, my eyes are my own private business, thanks very much. Now why don't you get a move on and stamp these library books. *(He puts some books on the table.)*

Doc   But Mr Henning . . .

Patient   *(getting up and groping round walls to the door)* I don't know . . . the library system isn't what it used to be . . .

Doc   *(shrugs his shoulders and shakes his head. Outside there is the sound of a horn blaring, a screech of brakes and a loud cry.)* There's no helping some people!

God can get us into shape

Beforehand prepare a card stencil shape of a circle. Draw the circle outline properly, but when you cut out the circle, make sure it has some very obvious misshapen parts, so that it looks something like this:

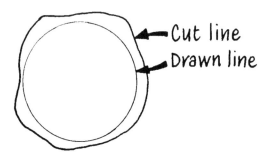

Have a flip chart or several large sheets of paper and a thick felt-tip pen ready. Start by explaining that as part of a visual aid today you need to draw a circle, so you've made a stencil to make that easier. Proceed to draw round the stencil and then express your disappointment that the circle isn't any good. Never mind, you can start again and do it properly on a fresh sheet of paper. Unfortunately, this shape goes wrong as well. Ask someone to try using the stencil and see if they can make it work.

When they can't, get people to explain why the circle keeps going wrong. (The stencil is the wrong shape; every time it's used, the misshapes will go on happening.) We sometimes feel rather like this – however hard we try, we find we go on making the same mistakes, messing things up in our lives again and again. We can't seem to help it. However hard I try, I shall always mess up this circle if I go on using this stencil. We need to make a new stencil for it to work properly, and in our lives we need to be made new so that we can't help but live loving, beautiful lives.

Ask a good cutter-outer to put things right, then try

again. (Hopefully, this will be successful!) Admire the results of using a stencil which has been made new. In the same way, our lives will start to show good results when we allow God to sort us out. He works on us gradually, every day throughout our lifetime, and as he works on us and renews us, we start emerging as the person God intended us to be.

God sets us free

Beforehand organise some prison bars. This might be a large oven shelf or anything similar.

First ask for a volunteer, who holds the bars in front of their face so that they look imprisoned. Sometimes we feel imprisoned by our family background. It may be that there is a history of cancer in our family, or suicide; perhaps there has been an alcoholic, or someone with mental illness; perhaps, however old we are now, we still remember a childhood experience of being intensely disliked, ignored or abused in some way. These things can imprison us and make us feel frightened and sad – as if we are partly to blame for their poor health, their sin or their weakness, and however sensibly we try to shake that off, it keeps hold of us.

The wonderful news of our God is that he holds no one of us guilty for what happened to our ancestors; Jesus can set you free from all that sadness and fear (take the bars away), so that you can live again and enjoy the life God has given you.

Now once you are out, you are free.

So if this person feels like killing me, does that mean he can? (No!) Why no? As God behaves to him – respecting and loving him – he needs to behave to others, so as to preserve their freedom as well. We can't delight in God forgiving us and then rush out and criticise someone else!

We might hear this and think we know all about this teaching already. But think again – what about when we discuss the service afterwards; do we only mention the boring bits, laugh over the organist's mistakes and huddle with our own friends? And when those around us are using God's name as a swear word, what do we do? (A hint – if you have got into the habit of swearing like this yourself, start turning it into a prayer as you say it.)

God sets us free; let's enjoy that to the full – remember to pass it on.

GOD'S WAY

God's way or ours?

Start by showing everyone how you have spoilt something by using it to do what it wasn't designed for – such as a knife for a screwdriver, or scissors as wire cutters. As we are made like God, and God is loving, we only feel that deep-down sense of peace and rightness when we are using our bodies, minds and spirits in the way they were designed to be used.

Now arrange two teams of three people (mixed in age and character) rather like a quiz show. Have each team holding their team name: THE GOD SQUAD and THE SELF SET. Ask a volunteer to be a Christian in the street, on his journey through life. He walks from the back to the front, and every so often you tell him to stop to sort out a problem. Have the first problem read out clearly, then ask each team what their advice would be. The Christian then decides which to accept, and the congregation can express their approval or not by clapping or groaning. Then he continues on his journey until the next problem and so on. It will be best if you think up situations pertinent to your congregation, but here are some suggestions to get you going:

1 The TV news shows a famine and you have just received your pay packet.

2 Your brother/sister has messed up your favourite tape.

3 The grass needs cutting but your friends are round.

4 You're gasping for a drink, and find a purse lying on the pavement.

In conclusion, make the point that if we say we're Christians it must affect the way be behave, but that even if we choose wrongly sometimes, God can still bring some good from the resulting situation.

God's building programme

You will need a lot of children's building bricks – separate and/or interlocking ones. Also make a stand-up notice in thin card which says on it: Our God rebuilds and restores us.

First tip all the bricks out on to the floor in front of everyone, and remind them of the rubble of stones which was all that was left of Solomon's glorious temple when the exiles returned to Jerusalem. Ask people to turn to someone near them and tell one another how they would feel in that situation. Now ask for two or three very young people who enjoy building. Set them to work creating a magnificent building, arranging them to face the congregation so that everyone can watch the building progressing. Ask them to carry on building while you talk. Explain how God responded to his people's feelings of sadness/depression/despair/hopelessness, etc., by speaking words of encouragement through his prophet, Haggai.

In a way the temple, so beautifully planned and made, and now in ruins, was rather like humanity – also beautifully planned and made, but also ruined through evil.

God decided on an extremely costly restoration plan: he sent his only Son into the world to put things right from the inside. Through Jesus Christ living in us we are once again restored to the lovely relationship we were meant to have with God. Like living stones, we are all being built up into God's temple – and the temple is a place for God to live in. God is not far away somewhere, but right here in and amongst us now.

Thank the builders and place the notice beside their building.

Choosing God's way

Have ready a musical instrument, such as a violin or trumpet – it needs to be quite a bulky one; a set of football gear, including a football; a large basket of fruit; six envelopes, three of which are labelled GOD'S WAY and the others MY OWN WAY. I will explain what messages are in which envelopes as we go along.

Introduce three volunteers who will be helping with this week's teaching, and explain that God always equips us for any job he wants us to do, but somehow, we often get it wrong.

Perhaps God gives us a musical gift (give the first person the musical instrument). Then we have a choice – are we going to do things God's way or our own way? The person can choose either envelope to open, and whichever one isn't chosen is opened afterwards so that both possibilities are seen.

GOD'S WAY: Use your musical gift to cheer people up and lead them in worship.

MY OWN WAY: Not bother to practise and never play for anyone.

One way gives a blessing to many, the other wastes the gift.

Now provide the second person with all the football equipment, saying as you do so that God may train us for quite a specialised job – perhaps for helping drug addicts through living with an addict in our family. When the person is all set up, choose which way to go.

GOD'S WAY: Play football for the school.

MY OWN WAY: Go swimming.

We sometimes decide to go our own way, completely ignore the gifts God has given us, and rush off instead to do something for which we are not equipped at all. Then we wonder why it all fails.

Give the last person a large basket of fruit, showing everyone how delicious all the fruit looks. Which envelope will be chosen?

GOD'S WAY: Give some fruit to people in the church who would really like some.

MY OWN WAY: Eat so much that you get tummy ache and let the rest go mouldy.

Sometimes God gives us gifts which feel very nice, and instead of using them as he intends – to share with others – we get greedy and hang on to them.

Finally, let the last person do things God's way, and share out the fruit among the congregation.

God's hidden agenda

Begin by asking people to forget they know the end of the story of Joshua and the battle of Jericho, and imagine what an unusual set of instructions they must have seemed for taking the city. A bit like being told to walk round your car shouting loudly if you've forgotten your car keys. Perhaps the soldiers thought Joshua was going mad. And yet God knew what he was doing; he knew that the walls weren't as secure as they might have been, and through prayer he allowed Joshua to use this hidden information.

We are used to interpreting things. Show some travel brochures and ask two people to come to the front. One reads an expression you might find inside, and the other reads out what we know it really means:

cosy = cramped

quaint and traditional = the plumbing doesn't work

very new hotel = building loudly in progress

sea view from some rooms = sea view from the bathroom

Sometimes we think we have the same agenda as others, but in fact we haven't. Ask two adults and two children to read this out.

Adults	We go for the children's sake.
Children	We go because we're told to.
Adults	It's a nice rest for us all.
Children	They sleep on the beach all day.
Adults	They loved all the animals at the farm.
Children	We loved the slot machine – if you wiggle it you get an extra chocolate bar.

The more we spend time with one another and listen to one another, the less misunderstanding there will be. And it's the same with God. Our ideas are often different from his.

Our idea might be: If I catch this bus I'll be home extra

early. But God's idea might be: If she misses this bus she'll meet Mrs. Merry and be able to help her with her shopping bags.

Our idea might be: If I don't pass my driving test this time I can always try again – I'm not going to kill myself over it. But God's idea might be: If he does pass this time he'll drive Terry and Pete to Scotland and meet his future wife.

Our idea might be: If I commit myself to a Bible study I'll miss my favourite TV programme, and anyway, I'm too shy. But God's idea might be: If she goes to a Bible study I'll be able to help her sort out her shyness, and give her a lifelong friend who will look after her when her mother dies.

Our idea might be: If I make that phone call and he doesn't even remember me I shall look a complete idiot. But God's idea might be: He needs reassurance and encouragement, and she is the most appropriate person to give it – this phone call will stop him falling apart. So if as you pray, God's ideas come to you, be prepared to act on them.

God's music

Beforehand either ask the music group to prepare a short SATB hymn, chant or anthem, or ask three or four instrumentalists to prepare a short piece of music.

First remind everyone that although they are here partly because they chose to come, they are also here because God chose for them to be here, and people praying for them opened the way for God's will to be fufilled.

Ask everyone to sit back and enjoy the prepared music. That is the composer's original plan accomplished, but a lot of people were involved in enabling the composer's ideas to turn into the music which helps us worship. There was the composer, perhaps the composer's teachers, the publisher and the editor, the person at the warehouse who sent his score to the shops, the sales person, and our music director, even before we reach the actual performers. (Have different people to stand out as you mention each job.)

All this is like the way God prepared the ground for the coming of Jesus, right through from Abraham, and including Samuel, who grew up to anoint David as king.

But God also harmonises; he brings things together in the best possible way for everyone. We can get some idea of this if we hear just one strand of the music on its own (just the tenor part, for instance). It's interesting but not riveting! Try another part on its own. There may be times of silence in the separate parts when nothing seems to be happening, just as our prayers sometimes don't seem to be answered, but in fact if there weren't those silences, the whole piece of music wouldn't blend as well as it does.

Ask everyone to listen to the music again, noticing the harmony and remembering how we really can trust God to fulfill his plans in the best way for us.

The covenant

Prepare beforehand a large card with the word COVENANT written on it. Cut the card into two sections along the middle.

Talk about when we go to see plays or films and find we're sitting right behind someone tall, or the row we're in is so far back that we can't see very much at all. We bend our necks to see through the gaps and, just as we catch a glimpse of all the action, someone in front bends over to talk to their friend so that all we see is the back of their heads!

In Exodus 24 we hear about Moses and the people of Israel catching just a glimpse of God's glory on the mountain at the time of God giving the Law and making a covenant with his people. Give out the two pieces of card to two people and ask them to stand one on either side of you, so that everyone can see the cards. Explain what a covenant is by showing how both parties promise something to the other and so both parts need to be kept. When both sides promise (the card pieces are brought together) it makes a covenant; if one party breaks their side of the promise (one person takes their section away) then they are breaking the covenant.

God promised to protect and look after his chosen people, and the people promised to keep God's Law.

Although God always keeps his promise because he is always faithful, people aren't as good at keeping their promise. Sometimes we get so many things in our lives between us and God that they block us off from seeing him clearly. We need to clear away some of those things in our lives so that we get more than a glimpse of God's glory – we need to seek him out so that we get to know him really well and can enjoy his company, as Moses did.

Rainbows and promises

Beforehand prepare this puzzle on an OHP acetate, or on a large display sheet of paper. Alternatively the puzzle can be reproduced on the handout and given to everyone as they come in.

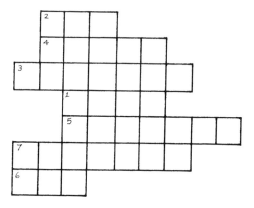

Today's talk will be interspersed with clues to the puzzle. The order of solving the clues is important.

1   (For a Brownie/Cub/Junior to answer.) Who did God tell to build a large boat?

    As you write in the answer, remind everyone of the wickedness of the people, and God's decision to clean things up, keeping Noah and his family safe because Noah was not doing what everyone else did, but doing what he knew was right in God's eyes.

2   (For a Mum/Dad/Uncle/Auntie to answer.) What was Noah's boat called?

    As you write the answer, you can tell them that the other place this word is used is for the basket Moses was put in when he was a baby. The same people may be able to think of what these two events have in common.

3   (For anyone under seven.) What did Noah take into the ark with him?

(They may well say particular sorts of animals. This is fine.)
When you've had a few suggestions, and if no one has yet said
animals, just gather the ideas together and write in animals
to cover them all.

4   (For Grandads/Grandmas/anyone eligible for a pension.)
    What did the ark float on?
    Point out how the very water which destroyed everything evil
    kept Noah, his family and the animals safe.

5   (For clever people to answer.) When else in the Bible do
    we find water used as a sign that an old, bad life is being
    drowned, and yet through this drowning, a person's life
    is saved?
    Explain that all baptisms used to involve getting totally wet,
    and that helps us understand the symbol of water. When we
    are baptised in the name of Jesus, all our previous sin is
    drowned and destroyed. As we come up out of the water, we
    are born to a completely new life in Jesus.

6   (For anyone who ate toast for breakfast.) What was the
    word you said before 'life in Jesus'?
    If no one gets this first time, repeat the previous sentence
    about being born into a new life in Jesus. Obviously no one
    was listening the first time! Explain how this new life is a free
    gift to us, and we can't ever earn it. What we do have to do is
    receive it and use it.

7   (For anyone who came to church on wheels.) When God
    makes one of these he always keeps it. What is it?
    When Noah and the animals were safe, God made a promise
    that he would never destroy the earth. As a sign of this promise
    he used . . . (direct everyone's attention to the vertical word)
    . . . the rainbow. Whenever we see a rainbow we can remember
    God's promise to take care of us.

God is our best guide

First ask for an intrepid explorer and blindfold the valiant person who volunteers. Now set out an obstacle course which ends with building a tower of three cartons. The course might have chairs to block the way, something to go under or over and the three cartons at the far end, which are to be brought through the obstacles one by one.

Ask for three other volunteers and explain to the explorer that s/he can choose any one of these guides to help them build the tower by going through the obstacle course. The first guide is blindfold and has his legs tied together. The second guide can see but can only see the place where the carton tower will be built. The third guide can see and is able to move around wherever she likes. The big question is . . . *which guide will the explorer choose?*

Before the explorer chooses, let everyone tell someone near them which guide they would choose and why. Then ask the explorer to decide, and set them off, timing their task to create urgency.

Afterwards explain how God is like the guide who can see and move anywhere he likes. This makes him by far the wisest choice in our lives, because he can see the whole situation, he knows where we are and what our limitations and weaknesses are. He can come alongside us and help us through even the most frightening, or difficult times in our lives.

JESUS

From Moses to Jesus

Rake out some nativity clothes so that you can dress a volunteer up as Moses. (Don't say yet that it's Moses.) When he is dressed up give Moses a label to wear around his neck so everyone knows who he is. Ask Moses to stand with one arm pointing to a cross somewhere in the building.

Now show everyone a telescope (or long cardboard tube). Ask a volunteer to stand some distance from Moses and focus on his face. Suggest that everyone else can make their hands into a telescope and do the same. Make some comment about what a nice face it is – so good and holy that we could look at it for ever.

Now ask everyone to look through their telescopes at Moses' hand. What is it doing? (If they can't see it pointing, they need to focus on the other hand!) If everyone carefully follows the direction of Moses' hand, they should find it leads them to focus on the cross. They have all just discovered a great truth – that Moses and all the prophets, and all the holy men and women ever since, may have beautiful lives themselves, but they always direct us on to see God more clearly.

Unwrapping God's law

Begin by reminding everyone of the ten commandments. Have them written up and uncover them one by one as people say them. Point out how they make for a stable, secure society, now as then, so they are very necessary and good.

Now show everyone a very delicate glass vase, which you want to send through the post. Can you just put it in an envelope? (Do so.) Or would tying string round the envelope help? When it is agreed that you will need to pad it to keep it safe, produce some appropriate packaging and ask a couple of people to pack the vase really carefully.

That's what had happened to God's law – because it was so precious to them, people wanted to keep it padded with all sorts of detailed rules, to avoid it getting broken, which is understandable.

But when it's all padded up like this we can't see it and forget what it really looks like. If, when this package arrives, we display it like this on the mantelpiece it isn't going to be much use as a vase any more, is it? The authorities were so fussy about the rule not to carry your mat on the sabbath that they couldn't see that God loves to set us free.

Jesus fulfilled the Law by unwrapping it (do this) so people could once again experience its beauty and use it. (Put some flowers in the vase.) So – we need to keep God's Law and not make excuses about that, but not wrap it up so tightly that we prevent God's glory from being revealed in our loving behaviour, our compassion and our delight in setting people free.

Jesus fulfils the prophets

Prepare this crossword puzzle on the OHP or a large sheet of card.

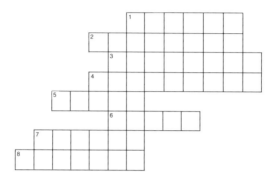

Give out each clue in turn; I have suggested who to allow to answer each one but do of course change this to suit the group. Make sure that everyone present has a chance to answer at least one clue.

Across:

1   (For uniformed people only)
    The plural of person.

2   (For those with long hair only)
    To say what will happen in the future.

3   (For those with short hair only)
    Truthfully.

4   (For those wearing green)
    Special and significant.

5   (For those with brown eyes)
    The real facts about something.

6   (For those without brown eyes)
    The name of Mary and Joseph's son.

7   (For those who like pizza)
    Christmas without the last three letters.

8   (For those who can/could skip)
    Fills with meaning; manages to accomplish something.

Down:
1   (Everybody)
    The hidden word in this puzzle.
    Solution to 1 down: PROPHETS

   Now ask everyone to help you with your sermon notes
by calling out the words as you point to them. Read the
message so that everyone joins in at the right places, like
this:
PROPHETS are PEOPLE. False PROPHETS FORETELL
what PEOPLE are wanting to hear, but good PROPHETS
FORETELL HONESTLY IMPORTANT TRUTH from God.
To FORETELL doesn't just mean to FORETELL the future,
it can also mean to speak out God's TRUTH even when
PEOPLE don't want to hear it. JESUS CHRIST FULFILS the
IMPORTANT TRUTH about God which the good
PROPHETS were able to FORETELL HONESTLY. In everything JESUS does, both during his time on earth and ever
since through PEOPLE who believe in him, JESUS shows
the IMPORTANT TRUTH about God's love for PEOPLE.
So who are PROPHETS? PROPHETS are PEOPLE who
FORETELL HONESTLY IMPORTANT TRUTH from God,
and JESUS CHRIST FULFILS it.

God with us in person

You will need some kind of transformer toy, a road map book of your country and a model car (preferably a sit-in one). Explain that you have brought along some Christmas presents to talk about.

First show the transformer and ask its owner to show how it changes from one thing into another. Like this transformer, God coming in person into our lives means that he can change us from being selfish into being loving; he can change us from being trapped by guilt and fear into being free to live abundantly and enjoy life to the full.

Now show the road map. Anyone travelling over the Christmas holiday will really appreciate having one of these, because whenever you get to a confusing junction which suddenly stops signposting the place you are trying to get to you can look here and see the whole picture, rather than just the muddy spray and tarmac around you. Now that God is with us in person our lives can be guided, and the best route taken.

Now we'll play a party game. It's a sort of 'Give us a clue' and it will help us remember what Christmas really celebrates. One word, first syllable: IN (ask someone to climb into the pedal car). Second syllable: CAR (ask the person in the car to drive it around). Third and fourth syllable: NATION (get the road map book and point to the name of the country on the front, or show the complete map of the area in the front of the book). Whole word, which means the great news that God is with us in person: INCARNATION. (In extrovert gatherings everyone can shout it. In more demure congregations, everyone can tell it to someone else.)

Jesus suffered for us

Ask two people to come out and stand at least three metres apart. Ask one of the people to walk down to reach the other. Was there any problem in that? (Hopefully not.) Now ask both people to get to you, only this time with one condition – they mustn't move. Can they do it? (No, it's impossible.) If they want to get across to reach you they will have to go on a journey to do it. Is the journey easy or difficult? (They can try it to find out.) They probably did that with no trouble at all.

But suppose the journey is made very difficult? (Tie all four ankles together with a scarf and walk away from them.) Can they get to me now? (Let them try.) As they are moving along explain that they can certainly do it, but only by using a lot more effort, and with quite a struggle. Stop them halfway and explain how being crucified was like a terrible journey that Jesus had to make to rescue us. In the middle of his journey people shouted at him to come down from the cross and save himself from the suffering.

Ask the people if they would be capable of untying the scarf and walking free. So could Jesus have come down from the cross, so why didn't he? He did it because there wasn't any other way to rescue us apart from accepting all the chains of our sin and carrying them for us, even though it made his journey so difficult. So instead of opting out, he carried on (the people can carry on too) until the journey was finished so we can all be set free (untie the legs of the volunteers).

God's loving risk

First ask for a couple of volunteers to start balloons off from the back of the church and ask everyone to try to pass these balloons up across the seats to the front without letting them drop to the floor or go backwards.

Then talk about how it feels to start at the bottom again when you change schools, go to a different area or have to change your job after being made redundant. Rather like the balloons, you feel a bit wobbly and vulnerable, and are not sure if you'll be able to manage.

Jesus, the Word, or expression of God, had been present when our universe first began. He knew all about the excitement of stars bursting into being, planets being formed and all the ideas of creation taking shape. But so as to put us right and give us life that wouldn't end, he was quite prepared to put all that aside and become a human baby, starting at the weakest level. God was willing to become one of the creatures he had made.

It was bound to be a very dangerous journey, because he was depending on people, and people can let you down. People can be dangerous, people can kill. (Pop the balloons.) God knew the risk he was taking, but because he loved us he reckoned we were worth the risk. The worst happened, and some people hated the goodness and love they saw in Jesus. Jesus allowed himself to be killed, but death couldn't hold the God of life. He came to life again having won the terrible battle against evil for us. He will be alive now for ever, reigning over us, loving us and living both in heaven and in our lives when we let him in.

The Resurrection

Beforehand cut a rough circle shape from a very large carton (such as will hide a small child). This represents a grave-stone. Also cut a number of teardrop shapes out of paper and leave one of these on each row before the service. Just before the talk secrete a small child behind the card grave-stone, holding a bunch of spring flowers.

First talk about times when we have been disappointed with a present or a treat, and how let down and rather flat we feel. The disciples must have felt like that on Good Friday when Jesus, their master and friend had been killed.

Sometimes we feel disappointed with God, too. Perhaps he doesn't answer our prayer for someone we love to get better, or perhaps things aren't working out for us in the way we hoped they would. Ask people to find the teardrop on their row and, as they pass it along to the aisle, to look at it and think of their own personal disappointments or regrets. Have a couple of people to collect the teardrops in a basket and walk up in silence to lay them at the foot of the cross. In a way, that's what was happening as Jesus hung dying there.

But Jesus couldn't be bound in death, and on the third day the cave entrance was found rolled away and Jesus was alive. At this point, roll the card stone away and the small child jumps up, holding a bunch of flowers, which s/he gives out to people all over the church.

Jesus shows us God

You will need a supermarket bag and two or three things in it which have distinctive shapes (such as a squash/wine bottle, a banana and a saucepan).

Show everyone the bag and ask them what they think might be inside. It might be all sorts of things, but we don't know because we can't see them. That's what a lot of people think about God – he might be there but they don't know because they haven't seen him.

Suppose I let someone come and feel the things in the bag. (Invite someone to do so.) Now they are getting some experience of what the things feel like, and that gives them a much better idea of what they are. All through the Old Testament people groped their way to understanding what God was like, and they felt his presence with them as they were led out of slavery in Egypt.

Suppose I show you the things in this bag? (Take the objects out and display them so everyone can see.) A couple of thousand years ago, God came physically into our world and walked around as a human person. His name was Jesus and at last everyone could see exactly what God was like.

Suppose I put the things back out of sight again. Do you still know what they are and what they are like? Yes, we know for certain because we have seen them. When we say that we believe Jesus is alive, it doesn't mean that we think he might be – it means we know for certain that he is because we have seen him in the gospels, we've seen him in the way his close friends live, and we've met him in our own lives and felt his closeness to us. Our faith is not about a list of rules, but about a real, living person who can completely transform our lives.

Jesus can save us

First ask everyone to imagine that someone has just stag-
gered into church and they've been shot. (You could have a
pre-warned accomplice to act this out.) Assure everyone
that this is only pretend, but if it happened, what could we
do? He might be begging us to help him and get the bullet
out (he begs for help) but we know that if Mrs. Eastoe or
Mark or David Stowe tried to put things right our poor
injured person would probably die (loud moans and more
begging for help). Can anyone think of someone who
would be able to help him? It would have to be a surgeon
at the hospital. So we would get the ambulance, and they
would get him into the operating theatre. Now if the surgeon can't be bothered because he's having his lunch and
reading the newspaper, our friend will definitely die (feeble
moans). But it's much more likely that the surgeon cuts
him open very carefully, sews up the bits that need sewing
up, and soon our friend is fine again and can go home.
(The patient thanks everyone, enthusing over what the
surgeon has done for him, and walks out of church waving
cheerfully.)

   We are all damaged and injured by our selfishness, our
guilt, our vanity, bad temper and so on. The only person
who can save our lives and set us free to live in harmony
with God is someone who is both God and human. Is there
anyone who fits that description? Jesus does. Will he want
to bother with us lot, though? Yes, he certainly does.
Because he loves us, he came to live among us and he died
for us. After he came to life again he went back to heaven,
and we are joining with all the angels and saints in heaven
today in saying, 'Thank you, Jesus – we think what you did
was wonderful, and we think you're brilliant, and we love
you' (or words to that effect).

Jesus is Lord

Beforehand prepare some sheets of paper in large zigzags –
computer print-out paper is perfect. On the sets of sheets,
write the words LEADING, ORGANISING, RULING and
DIRECTING, so that when the sheets are folded up you
only see the initial letters of the word, and when they are
let down you see the whole word. Fasten the top edges
with paper clips.

Begin by reminding everyone of how the people of Israel
wanted to have a king, like all the other nations did. They
wanted someone important, who would tell them what to
do, and ride into battle with them and so on. Samuel wasn't
so keen. A king might give them a hard life, and anyway, if
they had a king they might forget who was really in charge.
Who is that? God himself is really in charge.

   Ask four people to come out and arrange the letters you
give them into a word. When it says LORD, explain that
we are always talking of Jesus as Lord, and today we are
going to explore what that means.

   Unfasten the letter L so that the word LEADING can be
seen. That's one thing about Jesus; when we let him be

Lord of our life he will be leading us through all our difficult decisions and hairy, scary moments. Unfasten the O. When we ask Jesus to be our Lord he will be organising our priorities and the things we feel are important, so that our lives fit in with God's plans. Unfasten the R. When Jesus is Lord of our life he will be ruling over us; all the different parts of our territory will be in his kingdom and subject to his law of love. Even those rebellious outlying districts of bad temper, greed or critical gossip can be brought under his rule. Unfasten the D. When Jesus is Lord in our lives he will be directing us, with those tricky decisions, those awkward dilemmas and those nagging temptations.

So when we say 'Jesus is Lord', we mean that Jesus is Leading us, Organising us, Ruling us and Directing us every moment of our lives.

Jesus sets us free

You will need some lengths of rope, chain or thick string, a blindfold and a bicycle lock with padlock.

Talk about how we often tie our lives up in knots. They may remember having done something wrong and then having told a few lies to cover up. Or there may be some who have once had a row with someone and now dread bumping into that person ever again. Those kinds of experiences are rather like pieces of rope tying us up and preventing us from moving freely. (Ask for a volunteer who will help by allowing you to tie them up here and there.)

There are other things which chain us as well. Pick out a really strong rope or chain and explain how selfishness ties us up and restricts our movement dreadfully – we're so busy thinking about ourselves, our own needs and wants, our own rights and so on that we can't reach out to other people at all. (Tie up the arms firmly.)

Arrogance and vanity make us think we're so wonderful that they stop us seeing the truth about ourselves (put on the blindfold) and fear and guilt can make us too terrified to move forward (tie up the legs).

So we end up spiritually trussed up, living a compromise and never living life as fully as we could.

Jesus loves us and hates seeing us like this; he yearns to set us free, and the good news is that he can. When we hesitantly let him into our lives he will start untying our ropes of selfishness, taking off our blindfolds of arrogance and vanity, unchaining our fear and guilt (do this with the ropes, etc.) until he has set us free to live happily and love others. (The volunteer can caper around a bit to demonstrate.)

CHRISTIAN
DISCIPLESHIP

Chosen, willing and able

Beforehand place a pair of scissors under one seat, a sheet of A4 paper under another, and a piece of paper with 'It's YOU!' stuck with blu-tak under a third seat. Make sure that these places are filled.

First choose someone, by telling everyone that the chosen person will find a message with 'It's YOU!' written on it stuck to the underneath of their chair. Now you know a little of how Abraham might have felt when he realised God had chosen him. When we find God choosing us, we tend to spend far too much time thinking 'Why me?' and 'I expect he really meant someone else!' Abraham was happy to let God do the choosing. He just got on with being chosen.

Now someone has been chosen, you have a task for them to do. The task is to make an A4 sheet of paper fit round four people. Can it be done? Collect people's suggestions as to what is certainly needed before it's even remotely possible. (Four people and a sheet of A4 paper.) Sometimes God's plans seem just as impossible at first, and we're tempted to give up. But if we trust him, possibilities gradually unfold . . .

Does anyone happen to have a sheet of A4 paper under their chair? What about four people – are there any willing to volunteer? Now we need some scissors – anyone able to help? Point out how an impossible task is gradually becoming possible. Last we need instructions. Hold out an envelope and point out that it has to be received and opened up before it's any use, which is like praying and listening to God. Now the instructions can be followed so that the sheet of paper actually does fit around four people.

And here are the instructions:

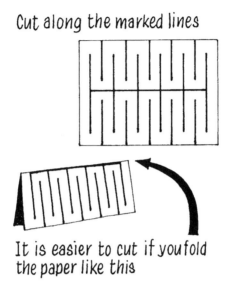

Cut along the marked lines

It is easier to cut if you fold
the paper like this

We may be asked to do what seems impossible. But if we
trust God he will lead us to the time and conditions where
the impossible can happen.

Follow that sign

Beforehand make a number of signs that are familiar to everyone. For example:

Show each sign in turn, and ask people: Where might you be if you saw this? How would it affect your behaviour? Now show this sign . . .

. . . and have someone carrying it round the building. Who followed this? Where did it lead to? Have the star carried round to where the crib is, with everyone following, or a representative group. From the crib show the last sign:

Remind people of how this affected John the Baptist's whole ministry, and let the sign lead people round to the font. This is the place where God leads us to commit our lives to him, ready to follow Christ and allow him to take charge. You can now use the Baptismal affirmation of faith.

The narrow gate

Beforehand prepare a narrow gateway. This may be a very narrow space between two pieces of card secured to chairs, two broom handles held close together by volunteers, or any other ingenious but simple method you think of. You will also need some big, bulky parcels, such as rolled sleeping bags, huge balloons, large cartons tied with string, etc.

First remind everyone of the narrow gate mentioned in Matthew 7:13, 14 or Luke 13:23, 24 and introduce your home-produced model. Ask for a volunteer to help explain Jesus' teaching about how to get through narrow gates. Load the volunteer up with all the bundles and parcels, either mentioning what they are or actually sticking labels on them as people suggest the things we often carry through life with us (such as resentment, I've-got-to-be-better-than-anyone-else, a cool image, I-want-it-so-I'll-have-it, me-first, and so on.)

Now let the person demonstrate what happens when s/he gets to the narrow gate. Ask them to try doing the things you suggest: first we might try to push through with everything and then get stuck; or we might try going in sideways, but that doesn't work either; or we may even squeeze through on our own and try pulling the luggage through after us, but because we find this is impossible we prefer to go back out again, rather than leaving the luggage behind.

But there's only one way we can get through, and that's by accepting that what we are going to is better value than all the clobber we have collected. Once we realise this we can say good-bye to it and leave it there outside while we walk quite easily into the life God has prepared for us.

Following God's instructions

First ask for five volunteers and choose people who have curly hair. Tell the congregation that you are going to commission them. Quietly tell the volunteers to go out into the congregation and each collect one person with curly hair and bring them back to you. When they arrive give each person one of these words, written large enough for everyone to read: I AM SENDING YOU OUT AS SHEEP AMONG HUNGRY WOLVES. Ask people in the congregation to unscramble the words and the people to arrange themselves in order. Point out that if the volunteers hadn't obeyed the instructions, the message you wanted to tell everyone would have been incomplete. Added to which they all look a bit like sheep because they all have curly hair!

The original volunteers heard you asking for help because they were paying attention and listening. When God chooses us and commissions us to do something in our life, we will only notice his call if we are paying attention to him and expecting him to communicate with us.

(Write on a flip chart/OHP: 1. Pay attention and listen.) Those volunteers stuck to their instructions, even though some people they asked didn't want to go with them. We are to stick to what God asks us to do even if it looks as though our own ideas might get quicker results. (Write down: 2. Stick to the instructions.)

Our message is a warning to everyone God sends to do his work – it may well be dangerous, hostile and frightening at times to be an active Christian. God very thoughtfully warns us first so that we aren't thrown by this when it happens. (Write down: 3. Be prepared for big trouble.)

Thank the helpers and display the message.

Conflict

Explain that living the Christian life can sometimes feel rather like coping with an assault course. Ask for some volunteers to help you set up some obstacles in a central aisle. There may be a heavy groundsheet for crawling under, chairs or a small stepladder to climb over, a dustbin sack to jump in and some thick gloves to put on before using a knife and fork with which to eat a mini Mars or a few Smarties.

You will also need someone to run the course during the talk.

Remind everyone of how Joseph was treated by his brothers. Could he have avoided that? Perhaps he could have been more tactful earlier on, but now he couldn't really avoid the conflict and had to just go through it. (The volunteer goes under the groundsheet.)

What about Jesus; could he have avoided the conflict and pain of being crucified? What did he pray for in Gethsemane?

He certainly asked if he needn't go through with it (the volunteer goes round the climbing obstacle) but he didn't get a 'yes' answer to that prayer. Going through that agony and carrying on loving those who were killing him was the only way Jesus could save the world. So he did it. (The volunteer goes over the obstacle.)

What about us? Suppose there's a fight going on in the playground or on the underground. Can we avoid the conflict or do we have to get involved? It's probably wisest to avoid it (the volunteer walks round the dustbin bag) because it could make matters worse and we might get badly hurt. But suppose you are living in a country where you will be imprisoned unless you deny your faith in Christ. Can you avoid the conflict? (Ask the volunteer to put on the gloves and try eating with the knife and fork.) Answering this question honestly is as difficult as what the volunteer is doing – we need to pray urgently for those who are in this position, that they might be given the strength and courage to do God's will even when it is full of danger.

Why?

Begin by asking various people 'Why?' questions to which they have probably got logical answers. (For instance, 'Why are you wearing scout uniform?'; 'Why do you wear glasses?'; 'Why are you sitting down?') Young children are always asking 'Why?' (Why?) Because as humans we want to make sense of the life we find ourselves in. When we understand why something happens we feel more comfortable with it – more in control.

But some questions are much harder to answer. (Like 'Why does the sky look blue?) Only clever, knowledgeable people can answer those kinds of questions. Some questions we can't even answer from research in the library or years at college, because they aren't head knowledge but heart knowledge. (For instance, 'Why do you love someone?' and 'Why did that young person have to die?')

There must have been people at the crucifixion who were asking 'Why?'. Those who had known Jesus healing people and loving them may well have been those who were most disappointed to see him refusing to save himself. Perhaps they felt frustrated that he wasn't doing anything to get out of the pain.

It may be that we can't see the point of some dreadful tragedy in our own or someone else's life, and our hurt makes us sneer at God: 'If you were really a God of love you'd prevent this or sort it out.'

Jesus on the cross shows us that he stays with us in the agony of the hurt, and will in some way, which we don't yet understand, bring good and new life from it.

Courage

Begin by daring some volunteers to do various things, such as singing a nursery rhyme on their own, walking round the church blindfold, or putting their hands into a bowl of custard.

Ask how many who are at school may be laughed at or teased for coming to church. (This is very common in many areas.) Encourage these people by recognising that they have been daring to come here today. Anyone who is teased or insulted at home or school or work for being a Christian is being brave, and Jesus knows all about their courage.

The truth is that if we are not being ridiculed, or meeting any conflict, it probably means we aren't living dangerously enough. Perhaps we've only got other Christians as our friends; perhaps we have arranged our hobbies and work so as to enjoy a peaceful life well away from anything challenging.

If so, we need to look at Jesus, and be prepared to make friends with someone who could do with some friendship but isn't well liked; or perhaps we need to check that our nice peaceful life isn't making us complacent – perhaps it needs shaking up a bit.

The armour of prayer

Bring along various items of protective clothing: marigold gloves, a cycle helmet, wellington boots, a surgeon's mask and some earplugs. Demonstrate these items with volunteers, and explain how prayer is a protection against evil.

Nehemiah and the returned exiles needed protection against invaders while they rebuilt the walls of the city of Jerusalem (Nehemiah 4:6-15). As we are involved with the building of God's kingdom we shall find those who scoff and ridicule what we are doing, those who deliberately break down where we are building up, and others who can take us by surprise and discourage or destroy. Praying keeps the channels open between us and God, so that he can supply us with all the protective spiritual clothing we need.

Difficulties

Beforehand prepare sufficient brick jigsaws for there to be one per six people. The jigsaws look like this

Have the jigsaw pieces given out to each row before the service.

First remind everyone how Pharaoh used his immigrant population for work in the building industry. It got his favourite buildings finished and it kept the people out of mischief. (He was not heavily into good race relations.)

We are all members of that nation of slaves, and we have to make bricks. We'll see which side of the church completes their quota of bricks quickest. Time how long it takes for each section of the church to have all their bricks 'made'.

Now emphasise the impossibility of Pharaoh's command by giving the same task, except that this time the pieces of jigsaw are taken to different parts of the church before everyone begins, so they need to be collected before any brick making can start. Stop everyone at the time they completed the task the first time. They will be able to imagine the frustration the people felt, being punished for failing where they couldn't possibly achieve. Some of us feel life is like that quite often and it makes people angry and resentful.

The people of Israel took their anger out on Moses, who talked about rescue from slavery but, in the short term, made life harder for them.

This seems to be a pattern of rescue, right through to Jesus having the pain of being abandoned by his friends and crucified so as to rescue us. So if we find that after being led to a deeper and closer walk with God, life starts getting extremely difficult, that's not a signal to give up, but to hang on, as it could well be the darkest hour that comes before the dawn.

Trusting God

Show everyone three things: a colander, a calculator and a calendar. Ask a volunteer to tell you which of the three things they choose to find the answer to 637 x 314. Ask them why they made that choice. Try to persuade them that the others might work. Try the sum on the thing they chose (which I am assuming was the calculator – if it wasn't, try someone else!) Are we surprised? No. Why not? Because we know that calculators do sums – we can trust them.

Do we trust God like that or not quite, yet? Think of who or what you go to first when there's a problem; *that* is what or who you trust most.

Why worry?

Ask everyone to turn to someone close to them and try counting the hairs on their head. (This will be easier for some than for others!) Ask if anyone can give a definite answer. Most probably no one will be able to. Pretend to be surprised, and disappointed that they aren't very clever this morning, then give them another chance with another question – really easy, this time. How many sparrows died in (your town) yesterday? Be amazed that they don't know the answer to that easy question either. Try them once more with a really easy question – who can add one day (not a week or a year, or anything difficult; just a day) to their lifetime? Show your disappointment and then explain how Jesus asked these questions, and none of his listeners could answer them either, so they are in very good company with the Galileans of 2000 years ago.

Draw attention to Jesus' teaching, that if we can't even do simple things like this, there's really not much point in worrying about everything.

Pick up a glass of water and ask if anyone feels thirsty. (If no one does, ask them to imagine they've just spent the last two days in a desert with the sun beating down – that should do the trick!) Give the person the water to drink and then ask them what their favourite drink is. Point out that water isn't their favourite, but when you're thirsty you enjoy any drink, without wasting time grumbling about what you can't have.

Worrying and grumbling are habits that we can get into and they spoil our enjoyment of this life which God has given us. Thankfully they are also habits we can get out of – listen to yourself during the day and find out if you're addicted to either of them. If you are, recognise it and allow Jesus to help you break the habit.

Singing when things go wrong

Beforehand collect together several scummy-looking cartons, and label them with such things as 'Bitter disappointment', 'Unfair criticism', 'Severe irritation', and 'Personal failure'. Also provide lots of dried flowers, stickers, coloured paper, scissors and glue.

Begin by talking through the Paul and Silas story in Acts 16:16-40, pointing out their unexpected reaction to a very nasty state of affairs. Then show everyone the boxes which represent those awful times we sometimes get when the very last thing we'd think of doing would be praising God or singing. We feel perhaps that it wouldn't be honest if we did.

Ask some people to use the materials you have provided to make the boxes beautiful – without actually mending the boxes at all. While they work talk about how some terrible circumstances are beyond our control, and we can't change them; like when the train we need to catch is cancelled, when we have to live with a relative who drives us crazy, or when we don't get the grades we have worked so hard for. They are like Paul and Silas's prison, or like these boxes. If we can fill those times with praise, those awful situations will become beautiful. It's not a question of pretending that we're happy and that everything's wonderful – that would be ridiculous. It's a question of getting in touch with God, feeling, with him, the horror or ugliness of the situation and then deciding to praise him exactly where you are, which may well be through your tears. That is honest praise, praise that recognises God's beauty and his presence in the dreadful as well as the easy, the painful as well as the uplifting.

Try it next time you miss the bus, get let down by a friend or the washing machine pours filthy water all over the floor, and make those desolate places beautiful.

Have the finished boxes placed around the church to remind people.

Holding on to Jesus

Beforehand, beg or borrow a ballet student or two from a local dance school and ask them to work out a short routine of exercises at the barre.

Begin by introducing the students, and starting the exercise routine at the barre. Then interview them, to find out about why they need the barre there.

As Christians we learn about all sorts of difficult rules to live up to in our lives, and if we try them on our own we'll probably wobble all over the place and fall right over.

But Jesus is saying that he understands that; he knows we will need something to hold on to for support, and he isn't expecting us to be out there on our own.

New life in Christ means having Christ and his strength to hang on to during the difficult times each day when it's very hard to do what is right.

Ask the dancers to do one of the barre exercises again as everyone thinks of something they find hard to do in God's way – like always telling the truth, talking about people behind their backs without being critical, noticing jobs that need doing or spending money wisely – and remembers to use the 'barre' of God's love and firm support next time.

Spiritual fitness

Begin by having pre-arranged people to set up a fitness training course in the centre aisle. This needs to be done quickly and efficiently, as if it is all part of the training session. It only needs to be very simple – perhaps a skipping rope in one place, a step or box at another, and a small mat somewhere else. Have three volunteers, of mixed ages, and ask each to jog to one of the positions. They are going to do circuit training, skipping with the rope, stepping on and off the box and doing sit-ups on the mat. Start the stopwatch and move them on to the next activity after 20 seconds so that they have all completed the circuit in one minute.

Why do people do things like this? To get fit/have healthy bodies. What might happen if you weren't fit and rushed straight into a game of squash or football? You may get an injury, or even have a heart attack. We need to train to be fit before the big match, not after it.

We know that so well, and yet we sometimes expect to cope with very difficult and challenging problems in our lives without bothering to get spiritually fit first. What might our training circuit look like for getting spiritually fit?

Incorporate the ideas people suggest, which will no doubt include reading the Bible, praying/listening and serving others. Put a small group of people reading a Bible and commentaries suitable for different ages at one place, someone praying at another place, someone with a towel, jug of water and a basin at another.

If we get cracking on this daily circuit training, we will be making sure we're spiritually fitter and better equipped to face whatever the day throws at us.

Don't just say it, do it!

Beforehand arrange two small tables to be available during the talk, each with a mixing bowl and spoon, bag of peanuts, bag of raisins and bag of chocolate chips. Also arrange for someone to read out the recipe, one step at a time. Stand at one of the tables, and ask for a couple of volunteers to stand at the other table. Explain that you're fond of nutritious snacks, and are really keen to make one this morning. Introduce the person who will read out the recipe so that we all know what to do. As the steps are read out, encourage the volunteers to do what is said, but don't actually do them yourself – just keep babbling on about how good the recipe is, and how clear, and how you understand just what it means, etc., etc.

When the snack is complete, let the volunteers show what it looks like and taste it. Now show your bowl, and let some of the younger children tell you that you haven't made anything at all. Protest that you must have done, because you had all the ingredients, and you listened to the recipe, and really agreed with it all. So what went wrong? The others heard what to do and did something about it; you didn't act on what you heard, so it really wasn't much good to anyone.

If we say we love God, but don't put that faith into action, our lives will end up as empty as that bowl.

Hear and obey

Beforehand get a box or case with a lock, and put a Bible in it. Lock it up and give the key to someone sitting on the end of a row, asking them to hold it out discreetly on the palm of their hand during the talk.

Begin by asking everyone to stand up, and then sit down again with their eyes fixed on you. They will just have demonstrated their faith in the chair still being there, because they were prepared to sit down without checking that the chair hadn't disappeared.

Give someone an instruction to go to the back of the church. When they get there they find a box which they can't open. Ask them to come back to the front, explaining as they do so that this is how we often act; we hear God's first calling, or instruction and then stop listening or looking. Explain the root meaning of obedience (instant and alert listening) and send them off again, reminding them to be alert, listening and looking, as they go. This time they will probably notice the key (reminding them to look, if they seem to be ignoring it) and can open the box. Explain how God keeps in touch all the way, if only we will be alert to what he is saying through events around us. When the box is opened the Bible is found. That's another way God speaks to us and helps us, but it only works if we read it!

We need to keep in constant touch with God; if we aren't, it probably means we don't reckon much to God's power, and don't think he's worth taking seriously.

Receiving God's gifts

You will need:

A few books – a mixture of popular and little known

A Bible

A Walkman

A first aid box containing some ointment labelled
  'encouragement cream'
  a bottle of 'refreshment'
  a bandage labelled 'understanding'
  an eye bath labelled 'grace to forgive'
  a Bible labelled 'handbook'.

The first aid box is wrapped like a present.

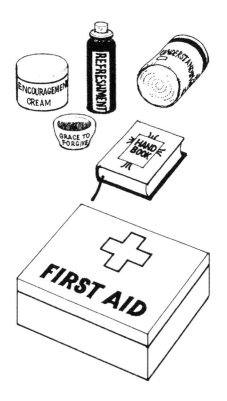

Begin by showing everyone some books. Involve their response – 'Do you like this one? . . . dislike that one?' When there is one they don't know whether they like or dislike, draw out that they can't tell you because they haven't read it. Show the Bible – lots of people have one of these in their homes, but if we don't read it, it's as if we haven't got one.

Now ask for a willing helper and fit them up with the Walkman, switching the tape on. Try to go on talking to them, but of course they won't be able to hear you. That's what happens to us – we don't hear God because we block out what he is trying to say to us and sometimes even accuse him of not speaking in our age. But if we really want to hear him, we've got to listen exclusively to him at least some time every day. (Turn off Walkman and release volunteer.)

And when we do read or hear God's word, what then? If we just put it away in a safe place and don't put it into practice, it will be just as if we haven't received anything. (Ask someone to offer you the present.) When they give it to you say 'thanks' but don't open it because it's too special. How does the giver feel when we do this? It hurts the giver and the present is no use to us, so he might as well give it to someone else. (Get him to do so.) Now this person opens it up and let's have a look at what's inside. (Go through the different items together, remarking how useful it would have been and how it's exactly what you needed.) So . . . make good use of what God offers – read his word, listen to him in prayer and put what you receive into action.

Natural Christians

First of all give some examples of how things happen naturally. Put some sugar in a drink and it can't help tasting sweet; have a brace clamped to your teeth and they can't help growing straight. Mix blue and yellow and you can't help making green. (All these can be actually watched if you wish – all those with braces can come out together and flash a silver smile.)

This principle works for bad things as well as good. If you drink 16 pints of lager you can't help getting drunk; if you put on skunk perfume you can't help smelling of skunk.

Since this is so, we will need to be loving people in order to behave in a loving way; we will have to be dedicated to serving God and others if we are to be able to act with God's character. Whatever kind of people we are on the inside will naturally show in the way we behave on the outside, so rather than working on doing things we think will impress people, God is inviting us to work with him in a transforming process from the inside – he can make us the kind of people who naturally think and love unselfishly, and enjoy our lives all the more for it.

The Christian adventure

Begin by asking about some of the adventures people have had, so that they share them around. (Just one-liners, like 'I was trapped in a lift once'; I got dragged along by a run-away horse', etc.) Have a collection of adventure stories, including books that every age group will recognise, and have amongst the collection the Bible, and *Pilgrim's Progress*. Read snippets of exciting bits from the books, including 2 Corinthians 11:25-27. Point out how Paul wasn't really the James Bond type, but as he went around telling people about Jesus' love for them, the adventures seemed to come and meet him!

That may already have happened to some people in this congregation. They may have mentioned Jesus and been teased at school, or insulted at work or at home because of it. When that happens, don't let it put us off – it's actually an exciting sign that we're on the right track, and are involved in an adventure story. Try writing it down, praying lots for people involved, and wait and see how God works in them. The Christian adventure is exciting, can be dangerous and should probably carry a government health warning! Try it.

Real faith

Explain that we are going to find out what faith is by discovering what it isn't. To make a point, have the word 'FAITH' drawn really faintly on a large sheet of paper.

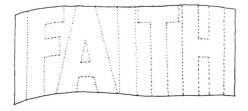

As each thing that isn't faith is talked about, some of the outside is coloured in, until the whole word appears in white, through the background being filled in.

Suppose you jumped out of an aeroplane, feeling sure that God would stop you getting killed; or you were sure that when you got up in the morning, God would have arranged for all the washing-up to be done; is that real faith? No – it's certainly odd, though. Faith in God isn't magic.

What about having faith that God will give us everything we ask, so we ask him for a bike or a new car. When we don't get it we can safely say that God doesn't exist. Is that real faith? No, all that proves is that God isn't a slot machine, which we knew already.

Or what about faith being a kind of wishful thinking. God doesn't really exist, but if we want to pretend he does and that makes us feel better, then we can, so long as we don't take it too seriously. Lots of people think like this. They think of us with a sort of pity, and wonder when we'll grow up. So is faith in God wishful thinking? No, faith would only be a 'let's pretend' game if God didn't exist.

Faith in God means recognising the truth that God is real, alive and active. When we have faith in him we are prepared to trust him to lead us, advise us, heal us and even use us so as to let more people have the fulfilment they long for.

Ask everyone to shut their eyes. Now they can't see the church around them. But it doesn't mean it isn't there. (Open eyes to check!) Sometimes we can feel God's presence very strongly, and that's exciting. Sometimes we can't feel anything but that doesn't mean God has disappeared – it just means we aren't aware of him at the moment. The more we listen and watch for signs of his presence, the more we will notice them. And the tragedy is that those signs are staring people in the face sometimes, and because they are so sure God doesn't really exist, they do not see him reaching longingly out to their misery, in love.

Perseverance

If possible, beg or borrow a cycling or rowing machine, but don't worry if this is impractical.

Start by showing someone having a workout on the machine, gradually increasing the resistance to make it harder work. If you aren't using a machine, have people skipping without stopping, or doing sit-ups. As they work, point out how in order to get fit we put in a lot of effort, and when the going gets difficult, we struggle on, and put up with it, because we consider the effort worth while.

Let the volunteers have a rest, and explain how we are also called to endure things in our Christian life. This may mean the daily effort to get on with someone in our family whom we find difficult; the constant battle against temptation of some sort; the regular, tiring care of someone who depends on us. Often the nasty part is not having any idea when this difficult part of our life will end, and if that gets us down, we are better off thinking just of today, or even just for this moment. God loves us, and will not let us suffer on and on in our own strength. He will be right there, providing exactly what we need to cope with the situation. And one last thing: God has promised us that we will never be tempted beyond our endurance, and there will always be an escape route if necessary.

All the way through

Beforehand get two sticks of rock which have a name going all through them. If you find these impossible to get hold of, use two Swiss rolls instead.

Begin by showing everyone a stick of rock and get someone to read what it says at the top. Break a piece off and give it to them. Surprise, surprise, it still says the same thing! Break this piece off and so on, until all the rock is given away, and we have found that the writing is there all the time, through every part of the rock.

Now remind everyone of Jeremiah, being thrown down the well and left for dead (Jeremiah 38:1-13). Before he went down he was telling the people God's message. Even when they pull him up, he's still telling the people God's message. (Doesn't give up easily, does he?) He's like the piece of rock (show the unbroken one), keeping to God's message all the way through, during the good times, the dangerous times and the painful times.

What about us? Are we God's friends just at the beginning, when we're all excited by the faith, or have just got baptised or confirmed? Or are we still God's friends when we get into trouble? (Snap off a piece of rock.) When everything is going really well for us? (Snap.) When life is full of pressures? (Snap.) When our friends aren't interested? (Snap.) If we are real friends of Jesus, we will stay his friends all the way through.

Waiting in hope

Beforehand get a kitchen timer, and one of those automatic timers which you fix on a lamp.

Begin by explaining how you are going to set the timer for X minutes, at which time the talk should be finishing. You are also setting the light to come on half-way through the talk. (Do this.)

Talk about the way things seem to take ages coming, because we want them so much – like birthdays, Christmas, holidays, pension day or tea time. Other things seem to come too fast – like telephone bills, exams or dentist appointments – because we aren't looking forward to them at all.

The early Christians were really looking forward to Jesus coming back in glory, and it seemed to be taking for ever. People who expected it to happen before they were sixteen, grew to seventy-five and died, and still Jesus hadn't come. It has been about 2000 years now, and he still hasn't come.

Now as soon as we start measuring the time for something, it seems to make us impatient. 'A watched pot never boils', they say. Because you know this talk will end when the ringer goes, you are probably all waiting for it to ring at any moment, especially as the light will remind you that it's all being timed. Peter told the people not to think God was slow in coming; he was just patiently waiting for the right time, and that might be any time. That's still true – Jesus could come again at any moment, on any day. All we know for certain is that he is definitely going to return in glory, and we can't give an exact time and date to it. Meanwhile, we can live our lives to the full, living the life of love that God shows us, and keeping in close contact with him through prayer and worship, so that we are ready when he does appear.

Citizens of heaven

If you have anyone in uniform present, ask a few to come to the front, one each of various sorts of uniform, such as a choir member a cub or brownie. They can sit down, and when you mention an activity they might expect to do, they stand up. Sometimes several people will be standing up and at other times only one person.

Explain how we do expect to behave in particular ways – even if we're not wearing uniform. A car driver needs to behave as a responsible person, for instance, or he might be a danger to himself and others.

Every citizen is expected to act reasonably, and keep to the country's laws, so that life is safer for everybody. We are citizens twice over (twinned citizens, rather than twinned cities) because we are citizens of our earthly city of Bromsgrove or Plymouth, and also citizens of heaven. So we have to make sure we behave like citizens of the kingdom of heaven, and be quite strict with ourselves about this, working at the parts we find hard and exercising the parts we manage more easily.

Our heavenly home

First show some colourful travel brochures, reading out snippets from them, and then talk about how nice it is to go home after a holiday, because home, for most people, is very special.

Ask everyone to think of the first home they remember. Imagine walking up to the front door, and looking in the rooms that they may not have visited in their imagination for a long time, or they may have left that same home this morning. Take them through various rooms, drawing their attention to things like the furniture, the kitchen window and so on, which will help bring their memories flooding back. That was the home they started out from on a journey which has brought them to Sunday morning, and the particular pew they are sitting in. Heaven is our spiritual home, and although we don't know any details, like the furniture and the windows of our earthly homes, we do know that it is a place of deep happiness and fulfilment, free from all tears and anxieties, lit with love and contentment. (Sounds good, doesn't it?)

If this was on the holiday programme, they may well be waiting now to hear the bad news of how expensive it is to go there, and how little chance ordinary people have of getting in. The wonderful news is that Jesus has already paid for us to go, and the fare was death by crucifixion, with the sins of the world heavy on his shoulders. What is more, we are not counted as tourists, but citizens of heaven. If we choose to walk with Jesus, he will bring us safely through our own death journeys to live in heaven. If we want, heaven can be our home for the whole of eternity.

RIGHT
AND
WRONG

The right image

Bring in an ordinary mirror. Also make a distorting mirror using a sheet of the very shining wrapping paper. It can either be stuck on bent card or simply held by two volunteers. Invite a few people to see themselves in both mirrors, or walk the mirrors round the church reflecting people here and there. Which reflection looks most like them?

Sometimes we are like good mirrors, whenever we reflect God's loving, by being loving to others. Or we may reflect God's forgiving nature when we forgive someone who has been unkind to us. Or we may reflect God's faithfulness when we are trustworthy ourselves.

But sometimes we are like bad mirrors. We distort loving into possessiveness; we distort relaxing into laziness; we distort honesty into critical gossip; or pleasure into greed. Worst of all, we distort trust. We are designed to trust God, and when we trust in things and people instead of God, our lives get twisted and misshapen.

If we get our trust in the right place, everything else will start reflecting properly and our lives will be very beautiful and very fulfilling.

Living as God designed us

Have an example or two of using something for what it was designed (such as a bicycle being carefully ridden or a sleeping bag to snuggle up in). Have volunteers to demonstrate the correct use of these things.

Now ask people to suggest to the person sitting near them what might happen if we used the bike to iron a shirt or the sleeping bag to skip with. Ask some stalwart volunteers to demonstrate, using a fairly old shirt and tatty sleeping bag in case of accidents.

Explain how God has designed us for living in a certain way – with God at the centre of our lives, caring for one another, being unselfish and respecting each other and one another's property – and it doesn't work very well if we live spiteful, greedy or selfish lives instead. We need to pray every day, keeping closely in touch with God who made us and knows us well, so that we can live out our lives the way he designed us to. That way we'll feel right and our lives will be a lot more useful and cause a lot less damage.

The ingredients of life

You will need to spend a little time making a cardboard 'machine'. Beg a washing-machine/tumble-drier carton and cut out a machine outline using a craft knife. It might look something like this:

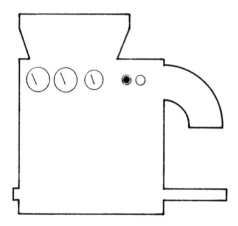

Set it up before the service, propped up against a table which has a washing-up bowl on it. You will need bags of flour and sugar, a tin of chocolate powder and a packet of chocolate biscuits, a couple of large potatoes, a bottle of cooking oil and a packet of crisps. You will also need an old twisted piece of metal (a scrunched-up metal clothes hanger will do fine) and a friendly, willing small accomplice to sit out of sight behind the machine.

Begin by explaining that you have brought along a machine which makes things. If you put in flour, sugar and chocolate powder (do so – just dumping the packets in, wrappers and all) the machine starts work with a low humming sound (which the children or everyone can do). And then the humming stops and out comes . . . (the child behind hands you a packet of chocolate biscuits) . . . these!

If you feed in potatoes and cooking oil, the machine starts humming and then produces . . . a packet of crisps.

Explain that our lives are a bit like this machine; if we put into our lives lots of lies and arguments and thoughtless behaviour and gossip (drop in pieces of paper with these written on) then by the end of our lives we'll turn out like this . . . all hard and bitter and twisted (the scrunched-up coat hanger).

But if we feed into our lives 'making an effort to be kind', 'forgiving people who hurt us', 'spending time with God' and 'reading the Bible' we shall naturally turn out a happy, free, loving person . . . (at this point the small accomplice climbs out and runs to give his/her parent a big hug). If we seek God and really believe that his love can make a difference to our lives, we're bound to become loving people quite naturally, and words and ideas will become increasingly in harmony with the God we worship.

Treasure hunt

Beforehand prepare three treasure maps of the building with an X marking the spot where the treasure is to be found. All three maps have the treasure in a different place. Where the first map leads, have a locked box with a bread roll in it. Where the second leads, have a locked box with a tee-shirt in it, and where the third map leads, have a large bunch of keys, which includes the (marked) keys to the other two boxes.

Begin by talking about treasure, and the way pirates used to bury their treasure somewhere secret and hope to find it later with the aid of a map. Explain that you have found three such maps and need three intrepid explorers to find the hidden treasure. Send the first group off, and as they follow the map, talk about how we all seek treasure in our lives, and our treasure may be some smart clothes from the High Street, or a new set of golf clubs, or coming first in our exams, or getting a really dishy boy/girlfriend.

When they find the treasure, and the disappointment of not being able to unlock it, explain how the things we rush after are often not as satisfying as we thought they would be. Send the second group off, full of new hope. They will also be disappointed just as people in life sometimes get. Send the last lot off, and when they find the keys, explain that this is rather like us seeking God; it's a waste of time seeking all the other treasures, because we might as well go to the one who holds all the keys, not just to our two boxes but to a rich, fulfilling life, inner peace and everything we need.

Children of God

Beforehand prepare two chunks of wood, which should be quite different from each other. From each cut a small chip. Also prepare some cards stuck on pea sticks and have a thick felt-tip pen at the ready to write in the signs.

First ask everyone what thing an ant might think of as huge. Then a cat. Then collect some ideas of what they themselves think of as huge. Remind everyone that all of these are contained in the mind of God and he is far greater than we can ever imagine. But let's have a go at imagining what God is like. Write the descriptions on the notices which people can hold up.

Now give out the two chips of wood and show everyone the blocks they came from. Ask a cluster of people round each chip to decide which block their chip came from. How can they tell? – By the way it feels; by its colour; by the grain, etc.

Jesus says that we are to behave in the same way God does – we are to be chips off the old block, and by looking at us and the way we behave, people should be able to recognise that we are Christians. So how will that mean we are to behave? Look again at the notices and they may be able to help us. If God is prepared to love everyone, whether they deserve it or not, then that's how we ought to be. If God is forgiving, we need to be as well. If God is trustworthy, so should we be to one another.

Look at the chips of wood again. If we're honest, we know we don't always behave like God. Jesus suggests that we recognise we are only chips and don't get carried away into thinking we're the block of wood. So long as we don't pretend we know all the answers he will be able to teach us through our lives to become more and more like him.

Real freedom

Beforehand prepare four official-looking files, labelled on the front in large letters, A, B, C and D. The information in the files reads something like this:

File A: A is very bitter at being taken prisoner, and vows that he will get revenge as soon as possible. A spends his time cursing the waste of his life, and makes life as difficult as possible for everyone else in the prison.

File B: B was very bitter at being taken prisoner, but then decided that he was only making his life worse, so asked God to use his imprisonment in some way for good. Over the year two other prisoners have met Jesus through talking to B, and their lives have been transformed. Many prisoners come to B when they feel down, because he makes them feel better.

File C: C is a gifted runner with an excellent physique. He lets nothing at all interfere with his running. Through this his marriage is breaking up and he never keeps friends because he is always letting them down. His parents are frail, but he never has time to visit them.

File D: D is a gifted runner with an excellent physique. He has offered his running gift to God to use. Now that D is famous, he often gets asked about his life, and uses these opportunities to talk about how important Jesus is to him and what a difference being a Christian makes in his life. As a result, many of his followers have been introduced to the God of love.

First have two people running up and down the aisle, labelled C and D, and two people sitting chained up, labelled A and B. Ask everyone which two people are in chains and which two are free.

Now explain that while that certainly looks obvious, we'll just check a few details out from their official files. Read out each in turn, asking/pointing out which ones are actually chained up, spiritually, and which are actually free. So our job is to live life to the full – however trapped or free we may physically feel.

Rules

Have a number of rules written out on large pieces of card. Choose rules appropriate to the experience of those present, such as:

Keep to the left in the corridors

No parking outside hospital entrance

Clear out pockets before dumping jeans for washing

Don't drink and drive

Hold up each in turn, asking people to work out what used to happen before the rule was made. Fill in the chart in each case, ticking as many columns as you like each time. Show how it is because we tend to be selfish/light-fingered/thoughtless that the rules need to be made. And in every case selfishness was to blame.

People were being:	Rule 1	Rule 2	Rule 3	Rule 4	Rule 5
SELFISH					
THOUGHTLESS					
LAZY					
LIGHT-FINGERED					
IRRESPONSIBLE					
FORGETFUL					

It makes God very sad to see us behaving like this because he designed us, not with *self* at the centre, but *love* at the centre – love for God and love for one another. When we live like this, according to the maker's instructions, we feel free and happy, and the world is a better place to live.

Helpful criticism

Bring in a bike in unroadworthy condition and ask a couple of people who have recently passed their cycling proficiency test (or some other well-qualified person) to take a look at the bike and say what's good about it and what's in need of attention. As the items are mentioned, write them up on a chart or OHP in two columns.

Now we are in a much better position to put the bike right. We are quite happy to accept this as a sensible way of going on for a machine, but start getting very upset if the same sort of things are pointed out in us. Instead of welcoming fair criticism as a useful guide to help us put things right, most of us find criticism hurtful, and get upset about it. Yet we probably know the criticism is correct – we just didn't want anyone to notice! And we do want people to accept us and think well of us.

So let's try a double-ended approach; to think of criticism as a positive thing and welcome it as a means to put things right; and to make sure that whenever we need to criticise someone, we do it sensitively and lovingly, talking to them about it, not about them to someone else.

All change

Begin by explaining that to prepare for the talk today you will need everyone in each row to sit in reverse order from how they are sitting at the moment, so that those nearest the centre will end up nearest the sides. Give them a short time to organise that. (This should create mild chaos for a while which gradually settles into order again.) Thank everyone for their co-operation.

What they have just experienced is an important truth – when God prepares his people for his coming, that is bound to cause disturbance.

There they were, sitting comfortably, and then they got messed about by you wanting them aligned differently. The people of Israel were living complacently until Amos came along and challenged the way their lives were aligned. John the Baptist's calling was to alert people to the way they were living and sort themselves out according to God's standards. When our own lives are challenged like this we have to set about checking the way we are living – are we in line with God's commandments and God's values? There may be drastic changes needed (as there were for those sitting on the ends of the rows), or there may be minor changes (as there were for those few who have ended up sitting in the same place as before). But either way we need to get up, spiritually, and take a candid look at the way we speak and spend our time and money; we need to look at our relationships and attitudes, and at the extent to which we allow God to reign in us.

Now, as they realign themselves again in their rows, ask them to do so in silence, opening up their lives to be realigned in keeping with God's will.

Inside as well as out

Beforehand arrange for a willing volunteer to come ready to do a quick hair or make-up demo on someone; someone else to give themselves a nice shave in public; someone else to sit and read their Bible and someone else to pray.

Ask these groups of people to arrange themselves where they can be seen, and start them off. After a while get everyone to think about which one is getting all smart and clean. The answer is that all of them are – the shaver and make-up person on the outside, and the Bible reader and prayer on the inside. We tend to bother more with the out-side than the inside, but both are important; let's try spending the same amount of time on each! Then we won't be in danger of being all nice and clean on the outside and all selfish and unloving on the inside.

Not papered over, but made good

Beforehand contact a local builder/decorator and ask if they would be willing to bring their tools and take part in a short interview during a service. (Well, why not – live dangerously!) Also bring with you a roll of wallpaper and a bag of paste. Start by introducing your guest, and say you've got problems with wallpaper peeling off and going mouldy, so would it be OK if you paste some of this new wallpaper over it?

As he goes through the stages of preparation and repair necessary ask him to show the specialist tools required, then ask him to tell you about the most difficult case he's ever tackled.

After this interview explain how we all have problems in our lives from time to time which are a direct result of sin. Like damp walls, sin needs sorting out thoroughly, not just covering over; if we try to cover over (as David did – 2 Samuel 11, 12), the sin and guilt don't go away, but make more problems. God is the only one able to sort our sin out by getting rid of it completely and making good afterwards, just as the experts do with walls.

First God   S . . . Shows us our sin,

then he   I . . . Invites us back to him;

but he   N . . . Never condemns us.

Blindness

You will need a blindfold, either a jacket with parka-type hood or a length of bendy cardboard with tie-ups, and an optician's chart with the letters arranged like this:

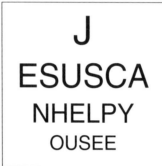

Talk about the different kinds of blindness we meet in John 9. First there is the man who had been born blind. Ask someone to help you by being blindfolded. (If there is a blind person in your congregation you could ask them beforehand if they would mind being interviewed at this point.) Ask the blind/blindfolded person how it feels not to be able to see, which things they find particularly difficult and so on. If you are working with a blindfolded person, take the blindfold and ask them how it feels to see again. Jesus enabled the blind man to see.

What about the Pharisees – the religious leaders? Were they blind or not? Ask for a volunteer and put on them the sight-restricting hood. What can they see and what can't they see? Explain how this can happen to any of us – we can be so rigid and concerned about a particular way of looking at things that we are effectively blind to anything outside our range of vision. Prejudice is like this hood; so is having a 'hobby horse about something' so that every conversation always comes round somehow to fishing, or the incompetence of a particular political party, or the trouble with young people today, or bad health.

Sometimes this tunnelled vision completely blocks people from seeing the good news of God's love. If they ask, Jesus can take those hoods off and enable them to enjoy full sight. But if they insist that they can see perfectly well already, then Jesus will be unable to help them and their narrowness is condemned.

Consequences

Begin by asking a couple of volunteers to run up and down, or jog on the spot, and as they do so, point out that if we choose to run fast like this there will be consequences. Stop the runners and demonstrate the way their breathing is much deeper and faster, and their pulse rate higher. They are probably warmer, too. All these things are natural consequences of the action they have been involved in.

If we choose to do something wise, like looking and listening carefully as we cross the road, the consequence will be that we have a far better chance of being safe. If you choose something foolish, like standing on your head when you haven't done that for forty years, the likely consequence is that you will probably damage your neck. We make these decisions all the time and how we choose will actually change the shape of our characters.

If we choose the selfish, unkind, greedy, or cruel way we will become selfish, unkind, greedy or cruel people. If, on the other hand, we choose the friendly, encouraging, honest or loving way, we will become friendly, encouraging, honest or loving people. What we become will be a consequence of what we choose.

Temptation

You will need a tennis racket, a number of soft, sponge balls or balls of screwed up paper and a large cardboard carton.

First go through the story in 1 Samuel 26, bringing it to life. Ask people what David might have been thinking as he stood there over Saul. What might he have been tempted to do?

Temptations are bound to fly at us from all directions all through our lives. Ask someone to help you to explain this by standing there as a group of people pelts them with balls. Sometimes the temptation is only slight (one ball) such as when you are tempted to kill your sister or brother. You know deep down that though she irritates you you wouldn't really want to do her any serious injury, so your fondness for her acts like a screen (they hold racquet up) and stops the temptation from getting any closer. (Throw ball so that the racquet screens the person.)

Sometimes the temptations fly at us so powerfully and urgently that even with the screen it is difficult to stop them getting to you. (Try this with lots of balls at once.)

What God provides for us is all-round protection. (Let the volunteer crawl into the large carton). If we make a habit of crawling into God's protection every day, then we will be better equipped to say 'NO!' to temptation. Don't try and fight off temptation on your own.

Be watchful

Beforehand make these two traffic signs from card, or draw them on acetates for an OHP.

First ask some volunteers to play a game. One stands at the front holding a stop sign and the others go to the back. They have to get up to the front without being noticed. If the person at the front sees them moving s/he shows the stop sign and they must go and sit down. While the game is being played, keep distracting the person at the front and see what happens! If someone thinks they can be even more vigilant, try the game once more, now that everyone realises you are deliberately trying to distract their attention to prevent them being watchful.

Make the point that sin creeps up on us like this, little by little. It's all the day-to-day acts of meanness, selfishness, unkindness, dishonesty and so on that gradually make us comfortable behaving with cruelty and lack of love, until we're completely bitter, cynical and destructive people. Jesus warns us to be watchful, so we can stop (show the stop sign) bad habits before they get very far.

The trouble is that Satan doesn't like us being watchful and will try to distract us, often in ways which seem very nice and reasonable (as you were doing). So don't be deceived by that. Make a point of learning what is right (show the other sign) by spending time with Jesus in prayer every day, and don't let yourself be distracted from being watchful.

The judgement of God

Have ready three dustbin bags labelled SODOM, YOUR TOWN and SAM. You will also need a grid of some kind, such as a cooling tray. Inside each dustbin bag have some cut up shapes of blue and orange card, making sure that the orange shapes will fall through the holes in the grid and the blue ones won't. Put many more orange shapes than blue in the Sodom bag, about equal in your town's bag and more blue in Sam's bag. Finally you need a clear blue sign with 'GOOD' written on it and an orange sign with 'EVIL' on it.

First of all introduce everyone to the three bags. They can imagine Sam to be either male or female. He or she is just a fairly ordinary Christian with 2.4 children. Introduce your town with any appropriate remarks and introduce Sodom as another city – the one Abraham pleaded with God to save if a few good people could be found in it.

Can we see by looking at these bags how good or evil they are? No, we can't. But there's probably lots hidden from view which the light would show up to be good or evil. (Ask two volunteers to hold the good and evil signs so we know what we're looking for.)

It's when God's bright love shines that we see clearly what is good and what isn't. When we do that . . . (tip the Sodom bag up over the grid) God filters out the evil so that only the good survives.

The volunteers can comment on how much of the city of Sodom survived. Allow God's light to shine on the contents of the other bags in the same way.

Choosing God

You need to get hold of someone who can juggle (however badly) with two balls today. If the juggler is really bad, rolled up socks will be better than balls as there is less retrieval time!

Explain that the readings have been all about choices, and the way we choose to live our life. We can choose to live life exactly as we want, buying loads of unnecessary clothes, sweets and luxury goods, yet unable to find more than small change for the Christian Aid collection. Or we can choose to live life exactly as God wants, sharing what we have with other people, being happy to help at home, whether we get paid for it or not, and putting all our time and money at God's disposal.

Perhaps we have already definitely chosen one or other of those ways; for many of us, we try to do it this way. (The juggler does his stuff. It's actually better if he keeps dropping the socks.) We try to juggle our choices, so that sometimes we are holding God at the centre of our lives, and sometimes self. As you can see, it doesn't really work. Sometimes we get into a muddle, all tangled up as we try to serve both God and self at the same time. And we never get to hold on to God long enough to get to know him and understand his will for us in our lives. Having self at the centre of your life will make you possessive and bitter, discontented and miserable. Having God at the centre will make you fulfilled, light-hearted and at peace with yourself. Juggling will make you confused. It's time to make the choice.

Salvation is God's gift

Beforehand, fix an apple or a bun on to a string.

Begin by setting an impossible task – who can eat the bun without using their hands while the string is being swung about? Several people can try, but make sure no one succeeds!

Then have someone butting into the game and saying something like: 'You're never going to manage that, are you? That's impossible. I can give you a bun myself, if you really want one enough to make a fool of yourself in front of all this lot!'

If the person accepts the offer, they are given a bun from the intervener's pocket. If not, try with the next contender.

That is like we often are with God. We waste our time and energy trying to earn God's love and save ourselves, when actually it's an impossible task, and he's happy to give it to us free. All we have to do is *trust* God and *accept* his offer.

THE CHURCH

God's family

Pick out two people of any age who belong to the same family and look alike or are wearing similar clothes. Tell everyone that they are from the same family. How can we tell? (Looks/mannerisms/clothes, etc.)

Now ask someone to pick out a scout/rainbow. How can we tell? (Uniform.) If I wore a scout uniform would I be a scout? What else is needed? I need to make my promise. As Christians we do that.

Could I be one of the Smith family? (No.) What if I made a promise? That's still not enough. For me to be one of the Smith family Mr and Mrs Smith would have to adopt me, and then I would be.

That's what God does. What is his son's name? (Jesus.) And God has adopted us as his sons and daughters, which makes us all brothers and sisters of one another and of Jesus, which makes us feel secure and comfortable and loved. That makes us want to behave lovingly to one another, because we're all 'family'. So we look after one another and forgive one another like Father does.

Members of God's family

Begin by asking various groups of people to stand in quick succession: brothers, sisters, mothers, fathers, grandparents, grandchildren, aunts and uncles, nephews and nieces, cousins, sons and daughters. Some people will have stood up several times – that's fine. Everyone should have stood up at least once. (If the congregation is wary of standing up like this, I find it is less embarrassing for everyone to stand, and then the different categories sit.) So in our human families we may be several things at once – a dad may also be a cousin, a brother and a son, for instance.

We are also members of God's family. God is our father – our parent – and, whatever our age, we are all his children. That means that everyone around us is a brother or sister. If you thought you didn't have any brothers and sisters, take a look around at some of your family!

What we need to do is to invite God into our homes – not as an occasional guest, but as a resident. We need to ask him to live with us. That way, our household will be filled with love, and we will find that we are able to treat one another with more love and care, and less irritability.

Chosen

Begin by talking about those times in games at school when the captains are choosing teams. Some people are always the ones left at the end which neither captain wants on their side. Others are fought over, because they're so skilled. Now, without mentioning what the team is for, ask a sporty-looking type from the congregation to choose a side, and have them all lined up holding a football, as in a team photograph.

Next tell them that they aren't actually a football team, but a washing and ironing team. Commiserate with the captain, asking if s/he's still happy with the people s/he chose, and giving the opportunity to change some members of his/her team if s/he wishes. (It will be interesting to see who is chosen now!) On a flip chart or OHP record how we go about choosing people for a job:

1 Know the people.
2 Know the job.

That way we can match up the needs with those who can best provide for the needs. And God does this all the time; because he knows us so well and knows people's needs so well, he can mix and match better than any of us. The trouble is, we often go rushing on to choose our own teams without really knowing what they will be needed to do.

If we look at the early church we find them taking time out to listen to God's ideas. They fasted – went without food – and spent a lot of time praying – spending time in God's company – and God chose two people to start the new mission who he knew would be best for the job. They were Paul and Barnabas. When you next have to make a choice or a decision, talk it over with God, and be prepared for him to put into your mind the name of someone you might never have even considered.

Filled with the Spirit

Protect the demonstration area with a groundsheet before starting the talk, just in case of spills. Have lots of buckets, jugs and mugs available, some empty and some with water in them.

Begin by explaining that all these represent people who go to church and are Christians. Sometimes, sadly, people may know all about Jesus, when he lived and what was and wasn't written about him, what everything in church is called and so on, but they are empty inside (tip the jug up). If anyone goes to them for a drink of God's love (try it), the person needing the drink will go away thirsty – they won't be able to get refreshed or comforted or healed or loved because the person they thought could help them is all dried up inside.

Let's try another Christian. (Try another container.) That's much better – this Christian is full of the loving Spirit of God so the thirsty person will come into close contact with God's love through them.

Look at all the different shapes of containers. We don't have to be a special shape of Christian to qualify. We may be simple or dramatic (choose containers to emphasise this), tall or short, Evangelical or Catholic. God is delighted to pour his Spirit into all of these, but one thing is necessary for all of us: we need to go to the source to be filled. We need to tell God that we want him to fill us with his living Spirit, and when he starts to, we need to keep ourselves open so that he can. He may fill us full in a rush, or he may gently fill us bit by bit; however he chooses to do it will be the very best way for us.

Sharing the workload

Beforehand, arrange for two piles of extremely bulky, cumbersome items to be put at the front of the church.

Explain that you would like these two sets of equipment/junk moved down to the back of the church, out of the way. Invite three or four people to work on one lot, and one person on the other. Invite everyone else to watch what happens. It should become apparent that the group of four found it both easier and quicker than the person on his/her own, who is probably left struggling and tired at the end of the operation. Suggest that many of us have felt like that struggling, weary person, when everything feels too much to cope with, and yet we know the job has to be done.

That's how Moses felt (Exodus 18:13-26), sorting out everybody's problems, and teaching them God's ways. The job had just become too big for one person to cope with, and that's why Jethro sensibly suggested the load sharing by other wise, trustworthy people.

We need to look out for anyone struggling on their own in ministries within our church, and offer to help. (If there are any particular needs, why not mention them here.) It doesn't make God happy to see a few of his children burning themselves out unnecessarily when there are others to share the load. Load sharing doesn't just get things done quicker; it builds up the love and fellowship of the church as people work together, encourages a deepening of faith and joy in believing, and guards against the onset of resentment and bitterness which are so often born of overwork.

Together with Christ

Have ready some pieces of card with these diagrams on them:

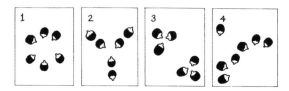

Explain that we often spend time looking at what is supposed to happen in life. Today we are going to look at what actually happens, more often than not. Ask six volunteers to make up the first diagram. Here are all these nice friends, and before long they start getting cross with one another and having arguments and upsetting one another. (Ask them each to find an adversary from within the group.)

Give one of each couple a red team band to wear, and give the others blue bands. Explain that all this blue-banded lot get together and feel at one because they have a common enemy – all those other horrors with red bands. (They move into diagram 2.) Then the isolated people with red bands find they have grievances in common and move together. (Form diagram 3.) Within their own groups they can feel really acceptable by being different from and superior to the other group – and can we think of some real life examples of this? (Such things as racial prejudice, gangs, exclusive sects and tribes.)

What happens when a strong outsider arrives on the scene, trying to make peace? (Ask one to join in.) What often happens is that now the two groups join up so as to fight the common enemy. (Move into diagram 4.) They have become united and put aside their differences, emphasising now what they have in common against the new enemy – they all have bands and she doesn't. Can we think of some real life examples of this? (A coalition government during war, or civil rights campaigns.) It's a very human way to behave, and it means a lot of people spend their lives fighting.

Jesus can help. He draws us all together so that no one is left out, and we all have a common enemy which is evil. At our baptism we are asked, 'Do you renounce evil?' and we reply, 'We renounce evil!' (Try this now.) Together in Christ's love and power, we are made one.

The grapevine

You will need a long piece of rope (such as a washing line), some shorter pieces of rope or string and a large pair of scissors.

Start with the rope coiled up and just hold one end. Explain that everyone is about to see a speeded up sequence of a grapevine growing. If the congregation enjoys joining in, they can make appropriate noises as the days and nights go by (such as snoring, 'wakey wakey', eating noises, yawning and snoring again, interspersed with rainstorms and singing 'The sun has got his hat on').

As the grapevine grows down the centre aisle, tie on branches (the shorter strings). When it gets to the time for fruiting, tie some volunteers on the end of the short strings. This should make it possible for the grapevine to stretch out quite firmly. Go up to one branch and cut it off or untie it from the vine. What will happen to these grapes that are just beginning to form? Explain that they will just wither and crumple (the volunteer can do this); the branch can't make any more grapes because it's cut off from the life of the vine. Remind everyone of what Jesus said: 'I am the vine and you are the branches. Apart from me [show dead branch] you can do nothing.' We need to check that we really are fixed firmly on to the Jesus vine, so that his life can flow through us and make our lives fruitful.

Witnesses

With a couple of people warned beforehand, stage a crime, such as a handbag snatch, in front of everyone's eyes. Then accuse an innocent person of committing the crime. S/he appeals for witnesses. Interview a couple of witnesses and let everyone vote on the strength of their eyewitness accounts as to the person's innocence. (Hopefully the person should be proved innocent – if s/he isn't, I suggest you go on quickly to the next hymn, or trade your congregation in for a different model!)

Point out how important witnesses are; if they have seen something and don't speak out about it, they are partly to blame for a miscarriage of justice. If we have seen what a difference Jesus makes in our lives and know that he really is alive, then we are called to be witnesses to that, so that all those in our lost and weary world may find the joy of his love for themselves. If we don't, how are they to know?

So, how do we witness? a) By our lives, b) by our words.

Going back to the crime that was committed here this morning, could those a long way off be effective witnesses? No. In this case that was out of their control, but being Christ's witnesses, the closer we get to Jesus, and the more time we spend with him, the more effective witnesses we shall be.

Telling others

Arrange beforehand for someone to be wearing their coat or sweater inside out, and for someone's bag to be mislaid.

Start by saying you need a volunteer, and choose the person with their clothing on inside out. Pretend you are rather embarrassed at having to tell them something, and then tell them about their clothing and help them put things right. Ask everyone if they think you should have mentioned it, or whether you should have kept quiet. If your sound system makes it possible, allow a few people to put their points of view.

Explain that if we can see something that is really wrong, and don't tell the person lovingly about it, they won't be able to put things right. And if we're on the receiving end, we might wish we did know where we are going wrong, or hurting someone, because then we are in a position to do something about it.

The prophets were shown what God wanted them to say to the people, and the ones who listened were the ones who saw God's word as an opportunity for growth, rather than as a destructive threat.

Now ask if anyone has mislaid their bag this morning. Ask if anyone knows anything about this. No one does. Point out that if we are in possession of good news and don't let on, then this person will stay worried and upset. Now the person who knows where the bag is stands up and tells the good news, and the bag is found. (A round of applause if you're that kind of congregation; polite smiles if you're not.)

There are lots of people in our world who are lost, and confused and scared inside or lonely because they haven't yet met anyone who introduced them to the living Jesus. And if you meet them, and don't share your good news with them, they will have to go on being miserable. Ask people to turn to the person next to them, and in twos and threes tell one another why they love God already, or why they are interested in finding out more about him. After a minute or two, ask if any four people would be brave enough to stand up on their own and say why they love God. Point out how difficult this is to do in the middle of sympathetic listeners, let alone with a hostile audience. We need to remember that being a witnessing community is not easy, and we need to keep close to God the whole time, supporting one another with prayer.

Worship and life

Beforehand you will need to collect six cartons of similar size and cover them back and front with plain paper. With the boxes arranged like this:

Draw a picture of three people on one side and write on the other: WE WORSHIP GOD. Write the same words on a long strip of paper which everyone will be able to see.

First of all remind everyone of how close Christmas is getting, and do a check on who has already made the pudding/got presents/wrapped them up/sent cards, etc. So preparations are well under way. But we need to prepare our lives as well, and how is that going?

Arrange the boxes in the right shape but totally out of order and explain that it is a picture of the lives of Christians. Proudly drape a long strip of paper over the boxes and ask everyone if all is well as they look rather puzzled. When someone says the boxes are out of order, say something like, 'Well, these words say they worship God so they *must* be right, mustn't they?'

What the prophets did was challenge the people who said

they worshipped God, but who lived as if they hardly gave him a thought. It happens today as well – we can get used to saying the words, but do our lives match up?

Ask a couple of volunteers to sort the words and pictures out so that they do match up with what they are saying. The whole thing can be viewed from both sides – when the words are really true, the people themselves are sorted out as well. And that's how it is with us – if we say we worship God, then we must sort our lives out so that they match up with what we are saying and, as we do so, we shall become more integrated, fulfilled people.

Welcome?

Beforehand arrange with two people from another church to come to your church as strangers today, asking one to dress in a way which fits in well with the people in your congregation, and the other in a way which might be difficult for the congregation to accept. This needs some careful thought! Ask them to come into church separately, and make it clear to the sidespeople that they aren't used to coming here.

At the beginning of the talk have a box with a closed lid. Is it open or closed? Now open it a little. Is it open or closed now? Then open it up fully. Is it open or closed? We are like this with other people and with God. With some people we are very open, with others we are a little open, and with others, we shut up tight. God's teaching today advises us to be wide open to God, so that we are able to be open and welcoming to others.

Now invite the two 'strangers' to the front, and explain the awful truth that you invited them specially to help us look at our own hospitality. Ask them how it felt to be coming in as strangers, and what would need to happen (or happened) to put them at their ease. This needs to be done with sensitivity, humour, and without any sense of accusation, of course. Point out how it is natural for us to find some people easier to get on with than others, and that as we realise God's love for us more and more, we shall be more and more able to reach out to others, even those who would not naturally be our friends.

FAMILY
AND
NEIGHBOURS

God and our families

On a large sheet of paper or on an OHP have two columns, headed like this:

FAMILY LIFE

The nice things	The nasty things

Give people a minute to talk in pairs about the nice things before collecting ideas on the chart, then do the same with the nasty things. Reassure people that all families have both, and that helps us learn to forgive, because we get lots of practice.

Point out that God used the jealousy and double dealing in Jacob's family to bring good in the end (Genesis 45). Joseph was able to help the family in a crisis and by bringing them to Egypt he made it possible for the nation of Israel to form in Goshen. Even the things which threaten to split a family apart can be used for good if we let God in to work. Family life is to do with helping one another. Do we make life easier for others in our home, or harder? Do we pull our weight as part of the team, or expect someone else to do everything for us? Talk it over with God and listen to what he puts into your mind over the next few days.

Today could be the first day of you changing things and helping to make your home a happier place.

The cost of love

You will need a bucket, a ball of string, two full bags from the local supermarket, a pair of child's trainers, a cheque book and credit card.

Talk about what things cost, asking the prices of such things as Sonic, a Mars, a 5-litre pot of emulsion, etc. Point out how the cost is known by those who have wanted or needed these things; our want or need pushes us to find out the cost so that we can work out whether we can afford it or not.

What about the cost of bringing up a child for a year? Let's check that out. It's something like 52 trips to Safeways (dump the shopping bags down) a couple of pairs of trainers, a chequebook full of club subscriptions, school uniform, birthday presents and a holiday, and a credit card bill of petrol for the chauffeur service. But that's not all – it also costs an enormous length of patience (unravel the string up the whole length of the aisle) and 365 buckets of love, a fresh bucket for every day of the year.

If we look around, we'll find quite a few parents who are more than happy to pay that cost for the privilege of a year's worth of son or daughter! That's how God feels about us – he is glad to pay what it costs to set us free from our guilt and sin and worry and fear, even though the cost is incredibly high – rejection and ridicule, pain and death by crucifixion. That's a huge number of buckets of love.

Neighbours

Begin by playing the theme tune of *Neighbours*, if you can stand it! Point out how the words are all about good neighbours becoming good friends – all very noble stuff – and yet most episodes are largely taken up with the feuds and grumps of those living around the Ramsay Street area. Quarrels, we suppose, are far more lifelike, and make better viewing.

Talk everyone through the Ahab and Jezebel 'bad neighbours' plot (1 Kings 21:1-24), where Naboth gets a very raw deal through the king's sulks and the queen's efficient cruelty. How do we react when people won't give us what we want? Learning to accept that we can't have things we want is often a hard, though very valuable lesson to learn. The more we work at accepting other people – whatever they look, sound or smell like – the less we shall find ourselves being driven crazy by them. We may not agree with what they do, but we won't be holding grudges, nurturing resentment or waging guerrilla warfare.

The law of love

Have a large sign prepared which says:

LOVE GOD
LOVE YOUR NEIGHBOUR
AS YOURSELF

and have ready a number of smaller pieces of card and a marker pen. (Alternatively, you can write the main message on an OHP acetate in one colour, and have another acetate placed over the message, with other colour pens at the ready for writing in subsequent messages.)

Ask two people to hold the sign so everyone can read it and invite everyone to do just this. Explain how this truth was shown to Moses, and through him to all the people of Israel. God wants this close relationship of love with his people, and that spills over into the way we treat one another.

Unfortunately, people being people, gradually lots of other details about the basic law of love crept in, partly to explain it in practical ways. Ask people to suggest some practical details arising from the basic rule, and write each one on another piece of card, inviting someone to hold it up, until the original message is hardly visible through all the fussy details. (Details might be such things as:

- go to worship twice a week
- say your prayers at least twice a week
- don't do any work at all on Sundays.)

Explain that some of the teachers of the law in Jesus' time had got over-enthusiastic with their detailed rules, and some of them had lost sight (as we have) of the real meaning of God's law of love. So what Jesus did was to clear away all these extra bits (do so) and reveal the law again in all its beauty. It is a beautiful thing to live lovingly – responding to God's love for you, and passing on that love to others.

Sharing burdens

Beforehand, ask someone to walk up the centre of the building when the talk begins, carrying a fully packed backpack, as if they are going camping.

Begin by saying we are going to be thinking about heavy loads, and when the camper arrives, interview them about the best way to pack things so that you don't put your back out before you start. Unpack some of the items so that everyone can see the weight-saving that goes on and the care that is taken in making the load as easy as possible. But it's still pretty heavy!

In our lives we are probably all carrying a load of some kind. A load is something which makes you weighed down, and we may feel weighed down from our concern about a close friend or relative who is suffering or is in with the wrong crowd. Or the pressure of work demands may weigh us down, or the strain of living in an unhappy environment, or the fear of a bully at school. All these things can feel like heavy burdens. For many in the world the burden is not having enough to eat, not being able to feed your children, not having your home any more, or not being able to get treatment for a loved one who is very ill. Some of these weights can be made a little easier by ourselves, but for most of them we need to share the weight with others, who can help take the strain. To do that, two things are needed:

1 For us to be willing to share another person's load.
    (Let a volunteer come and pick up an empty backpack.)
2 For us to be willing to let others help us.
    (The camper agrees to be helped, and together they share the load.)

INDEX

Index